Mallorca

DIRECTIONS

WRITTEN AND RESEARCHED BY

Phil Lee

NEW YORK • LONDON • DELHI

www.roughguides.com

Contents

Introduction to

Mallorca

Commonly perceived as little more than sun, sex, booze and high-rise hotels, Mallorca is – to the surprise of many first–time visitors – often beautiful and frequently fascinating. The island's negative image was spawned by the helter-skelter development of the 1960s, which submerged tracts of the coastline beneath hotels, villas and apartment blocks, but in fact,

◄ Religious tilework

the concrete sprawl is largely confined to the Bay of Palma and a handful of mega-resorts, and for the most part Mallorca remains untouched. Another surprise is the startling variety that characterizes the island, from the craggy mountains and medieval monasteries of its northwest coast through to the whitewashed towns and rolling farmland of the central plain – altogether quite enough to attract a battery of artists, actors and writers from Robert Graves to Michael Douglas.

▲ Mallorcan village

Catalan and Castilian

After the death of Franco in 1975, Spain was divided on federal lines with the Balearics forming their own autonomous region. One result was the re-emergence of Catalan (*Català*), the main language of the islanders, at the expense of Castilian (Spanish), which Franco had imposed as the only language of government and education. The most obvious sign of this linguistic change has been the replacement of Castilian street names by their Catalan equivalents. The islanders speak Catalan in a local dialect, *Mallorquín*, though they are almost all bilingual, speaking Castilian and Catalan with equal fluency.

Mallorca is the largest of the Balearic Islands, an archipelago to the east of the Spanish mainland comprising four main islands – Mallorca, Menorca, Ibiza and Formentera. As such, it straddled the sailing routes between the eastern and western Mediterranean and was an important and prosperous trading station until the sixteenth century when the Spanish dash to exploit the Americas turned trade routes on their heads. Thereafter, the island became a neglected

▲ Serra de Tramuntana mountain range, Western Mallorca

When to visit

Spring and autumn are the ideal times for a visit, when the weather is comfortably warm with none of the oven-like temperatures which bake the island in July and August. It's well worth considering a winter break too: even in January, temperatures are usually high enough during the day to sit out at a café in shirtsleeves. Mallorca sees occasional rain in winter, however, and the Serra de Tramuntana mountains, which protect the rest of Mallorca from inclement weather and the prevailing northerly winds, are often buffeted by storms.

Mediterranean backwater controlled by a conservative landed gentry, whose large estates dominated Es Pla, the fertile central plain, until mass tourism simply swept the established order away in the 1960s. Agriculture, once the mainstay of the local economy, faded into the background, and the island's former poverty evaporated: today, Mallorca's population of 640,000 enjoys the highest per capita level of disposable income in Spain.

▲ Mondragó beach, Southern Mallorca

Mallorca
AT A GLANCE

PALMA

Palma, the island capital, arches around the shores of the Bay of Palma. It is the Balearics' one real city, a bustling, historic place whose grandee mansions and magnificent Gothic cathedral serve as a fine backdrop to an excellent café and restaurant scene.

▾ Old town, Palma

THE BAY OF PALMA (BADIA DE PALMA)

The tourist resorts to either side of Palma merge into a thirty-kilometre-long stretch of intensive development that can be dispiriting. Nevertheless, there are highlights, principally the former home and studio of Joan Miró in Cala Major and the cove beach of Portals Vells.

▾ Illetes beach, Bay of Palma

WESTERN MALLORCA

The wild and wonderful Serra de Tramuntana mountains bump along the island's northwest coast-line, punctuated by deep sheltered valleys, mountain villages and beautiful cove beaches. Roughly midway is Sóller, an old market town, which is best reached from Palma on the antique railway, an extraordinarily scenic journey.

INTRODUCTION

▲ Serra de Tramuntana mountains

NORTHERN MALLORCA

Beyond Sóller, the Serra de Tramuntana mountains thunder along the coastline as far as Lluc monastery before rolling down to a coastal plain, which holds the lovely little town of Pollença, the attractive resort of Port de Pollença and a key birdwatching site, the Parc Natural de S'Albufera.

SOUTHERN MALLORCA

East of Palma stretches Es Pla, an agricultural plain that occupies the centre of the island, sprinkled with country towns, most memorably Petra and Sineu. In the east, Es Pla is bounded by Mallorca's second mountain range, the gentler Serres de Llevant, which runs just inland from the mega-resorts, coves and caves of the east coast and culminates in the pine-clad headlands and medieval hill towns of the island's northeast corner. The sparse flatlands of the south

coast are less appealing, but Colònia de Sant Jordi is an agreeable resort and home port for the boat to Cabrera island.

▲ Santuari de Sant Salvador, Serres de Llevant

Ideas

The big six

Mallorca has lots of hidden corners and a staggeringly beautiful shoreline as well as some outstanding individual sights. Two are monasteries, Lluc and Valldemossa, where Chopin and his lover, George Sand, spent the winter of 1838, and another is the magnificent Gothic extravagance of Palma Cathedral. There's also the train over the mountains between Palma and Sóller, plus the mountain village of Deià and the sun–bleached mountains themselves, the Serra de Tramuntana.

▲ **Valldemossa Monastery**

Amongst the island's monasteries, Valldemossa is the most enchanting.

P.98 ▶ WESTERN MALLORCA

▲ **Monestir de Lluc**

Hidden in the mountains, Lluc holds La Morenata – the Black Madonna – the island's holiest icon.

P.110 ▶ NORTHERN MALLORCA

▲ Palma Cathedral

The capital's most impressive building, Palma Cathedral is quite simply one of Spain's finest Gothic buildings.

P.51 ▸ PALMA

▼ Deià

Of all the mountain villages strung along the northwest coast, Deià is probably the prettiest.

P.93 ▸ WESTERN MALLORCA

▲ The Palma–Sóller train

This antique train provides a fine introduction to Mallorca's mountainous charms.

P.85 ▸ WESTERN MALLORCA

▼ Serra de Tramuntana

This range of rugged mountains bands the northwest coast and makes for ideal hiking in the spring and autumn.

P.108 ▸ WESTERN MALLORCA

Churches and shrines

Profoundly Catholic for much of its history, Mallorca possesses literally scores of churches and a scattering of hilltop shrines, where the penitential still troop off for blessings and cures. Most of the more important churches are Gothic in design, dating from the thirteenth and fourteenth centuries, but their interiors are largely Baroque, adorned by kitsch – or mawkish – religious statues and paintings.

▲ **Santuari de Nostra Senyora de Cura, Puig Randa**

Dinky little church perched on a hill and part of a complex that was formerly a Franciscan monastery.

P.131 ▸ SOUTHERN MALLORCA

▲ **Santa Eulalia, Palma**

Classic Gothic church dating from the thirteenth century and with a colossal high altar.

P.60 ▸ PALMA

▼ Nostra Senyora dels Dolors, Manacor

Well-proportioned Gothic church overlooking the town's main square.

P.135 ▶ SOUTHERN MALLORCA

▼ Palma Cathedral

Overlooking the Mediterranean, the Cathedral is the most impressive church on the island by a long chalk.

P.51 ▶ PALMA

▲ Nostra Senyora de los Angeles, Sineu

The grandest parish church on the island with an imposing bell tower.

P.132 ▶ SOUTHERN MALLORCA

▲ Basílica de Sant Francesc, Palma

Built for the Franciscans, this church has all manner of Gothic and Baroque details.

P.61 ▶ PALMA

Restaurants

Several million tourists visit Mallorca every year, one result being a superabundance of restaurants. Standards vary enormously, but almost every resort, town and village has at least a couple of good places and there's also a scattering of memorable restaurants dotted right across the island, nowhere more so than in Palma. The best restaurants often make use of local produce with seafood, pig and lamb leading the gastronomic way.

▲ El Guía

Traditional restaurant in Sóller offering a first-rate *menú del día*.

P.104 ▸ WESTERN MALLORCA

▲ Aramís

One of the capital's finest restaurants with an imaginative menu featuring the freshest of local ingredients.

P.70 ▸ PALMA

▲ Ca'n Carlos

Outstanding restaurant in the centre of Palma featuring the best of Mallorcan cuisine.

P.70 ▶ PALMA

▼ Es Racó d'es Teix

Wonderful views and wonderful food at this top-flight Deià restaurant.

P.106 ▶ WESTERN MALLORCA

▲ Es Turó

Family-run restaurant in Fornalutx offering traditional island food and great valley views – all at very reaonable prices.

P.89 ▶ WESTERN MALLORCA

Festivals

Almost every town and village in Mallorca takes at least one day off a year to devote to a festival. Usually it's the local saint's day, but there are celebrations, too, of harvests, deliverance from the Moors, of safe return from the sea – any excuse will do. Each festival is, of course, different, with a particular local emphasis, but there is always music, dancing, traditional costume and an immense spirit of enjoyment.

▲ Carnaval (Carnival)

Marches and fancy dress parades in every Mallorcan town during the week before Lent – in February.

P.162 ▶ ESSENTIALS

▲ Escolania de Lluc

The choir boys of Lluc monastery perform at Mass twice daily – usually at 11am and 7pm.

P.112 ▶ WESTERN MALLORCA

▲ Sa Firá i Es Firó

A town- and life-saving victory by the inhabitants of Sóller over invading Turks is commemorated with mock battles in mid-May.

P.90 ▶ WESTERN MALLORCA

▶ Revetla de Sant Antoni Abat (Eve of St Antony Abbot's Day)

Masks and parties and the lighting of bonfires across the island mark this saint's day, on January 16.

P.161 ▶ ESSENTIALS

▼ Setmana Santa (Holy Week)

During Easter week the island sees dozens of religious ceremonies – such as this ominous-looking parade in Palma.

P.162 ▶ ESSENTIALS

Castles

Subject to invasion and pirate attack, life on Mallorca has often been dangerous and the island's hilltop castles bear witness to those troubled times. Some of these strongholds – like the castle on the edge of Palma – are now easy to reach by road, but others still require a lung-wrenching hike.

▲ Capdepera

Postcard-perfect castle whose castellated walls clamber up the steepest of hillsides.

P.138 ▸ NORTHERN MALLORCA

▲ Castell de Bellver, Palma

Dating from the fourteenth century, this hilltop castle is in immaculate condition and offers stirring views over Palma.

P.67 ▶ PALMA

▼ Castell d'Alaró

The shattered ruins of this former Moorish stronghold occupy a stupendously wild location.

P.91 ▶ WESTERN MALLORCA

▲ Castell de Santueri

Long abandoned, the crumbling stonework of this medieval fortress glowers across the surrounding flatlands.

P.142 ▶ SOUTHERN MALLORCA

Late-night Palma

Every resort in every part of the island has a healthy supply of bars and restaurants, but only in Palma does the nightlife really hum, with a clutch of lively late-night bars and clubs. Here in the capital, there's something to suit every disposition, whether straight or gay, budget or expense account.

▲ **Abaco**

Ambitious late-night bar bedecked with flowers and serving fanciful cocktails.

P.71 ▸ PALMA

◀ DJ events

Palma offers regular musical spectaculars with well-known DJs often appearing outside at the Parc de la Mar.

P.56 ▸ PALMA

▲ Tito's

Established nightspot playing every sort of music, plus frequent live bands.

P.72 ▸ PALMA

▼ Gotic

Groovy bar with a candlelit patio and pavement tables, plus a house backing track.

P.72 ▸ PALMA

Ancient Mallorca

Mallorca is dotted with prehistoric remains, a remarkably varied bunch mostly dating from around 1400 to 800 BC. There are colonies of cave dwellings overlooking the sea, underground halls and chambers, cone-shaped rock mounds – *talayots* – that may have been watchtowers and several walled villages, most memorably Ses Paisses. The Romans occupied Mallorca in 123 BC and stayed for nearly six hundred years. Little remains from this period, but there are a couple of noteworthy sights at Alcúdia.

▲ Ses Paisses, Artà

Ses Paisses is the best-preserved prehistoric settlement on Mallorca and comes complete with its cyclopean walls.

P.136 ▶ SOUTHERN MALLORCA

▲ Teatre Roman, Alcúdia

This open-air theatre is the most rewarding of the island's Roman remains.

P.120 ▶ NORTHERN MALLORCA

▼ Capocorb Vell

The sprawling ruins of this prehistoric village hold no fewer than five stone towers, or *talayots*.

P.149 ▸ SOUTHERN MALLORCA

▼ Palma's Museu de Mallorca

This is Mallorca's most enjoyable museum and it holds an extensive collection of prehistoric artefacts, including this totemic bull's head.

P.58 ▸ PALMA

▲ Pollentia, Alcúdia

Roman Pollentia was once an important trading station and colony.

P.120 ▸ NORTHERN MALLORCA

Birdwatchers' Mallorca

Mallorca's diverse birdlife has attracted ornithologists for decades. The island boasts a whole batch of resident Mediterranean specialists plus migrating flocks of northern European birds which arrive in their thousands during the spring and autumn. The northern mountains are also a haven for birds of prey, the cliffs of the western coast are thronged with seabirds, the island's country lanes have corn buntings, warblers, nightingales and hoopoes and the island's wetlands attract a varied crew from moorhens and crakes to raptors.

▲ Hoopoe (Upupa epops)

Pigeon-sized, pinky-brown bird with barred head-crest and wings; breeding resident favouring open ground.

P.143 ▸ SOUTHERN MALLORCA

▲ Black Vulture (Aegypius monachus)

The most distinctive of the island's birds, this solitary raptor is a breeding resident confined to the northern mountains.

P.108 ▸ NORTHERN MALLORCA

▶ Purple Gallinule (Porphyrio porphyrio)

Strange purple-blue, hen-like bird, which is a breeding resident at the Parc Natural de S'Albufera

P.122 ▶ NORTHERN MALLORCA

▲ Audoin's Gull (Larus audouinii)

A rare gull, with an unusual red bill, this resident breeder sticks to rocky stretches of coastline.

P.118 ▶ NORTHERN MALLORCA

▼ Parc Natural de S'Albufera

The wetlands here are the best birdwatching spot on the island; the park has a dozen hides.

P.122 ▶ NORTHERN MALLORCA

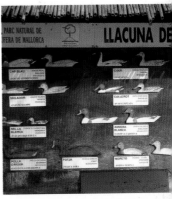

▼ Cap de Formentor

This cape is the breeding ground of shearwaters, Mediterranean shags, storm petrels and Audouin's gulls.

P.118 ▶ NORTHERN MALLORCA

Monastery rooms

Mallorca is short of monks, so short in fact that the monasteries of yesteryear are now maintained by secular wardens, who rent out empty cells, at five of them, to tourists (of either sex). All have lovely rural settings, four (the exception is Lluc) perch on hilltops, and, although there's an increasing demand for this sort of plain and inexpensive accommodation, they are rarely full. Reasonably priced food is usually available at these monasteries, but check when you book.

▲ Monestir de Lluc

The most visited and commercialized of the monasteries which provide accommodation, Lluc is also a major tourist attraction in its own right.

P.125 ▸ NORTHERN MALLORCA

▼ Santuari de Nostra Senyora de Cura, on Puig Randa, near Algaida

Simple rooms are available in this hilltop complex, which mostly dates from the early twentieth century.

P.150 ▸ SOUTHERN MALLORCA

▶ Santuari de Sant Salvador, near Felanitx

Grand views over the east coast and a handsome setting make the *santuari* an appealing proposition.

P.150 ▶ SOUTHERN MALLORCA

▼ Ermita de Nostra Senyora de Bonany, near Petra

No frills perhaps, but this monastery is certainly off the beaten track.

P.149 ▶ SOUTHERN MALLORCA

▲ Ermita de Nostra Senyora del Puig, outside Pollença

With panoramic views over the coastline, this old monastery enjoys a spectacular setting.

P.124 ▶ NORTHERN MALLORCA

Gastronomic Mallorca

Traditional Mallorcan food is a peasant cuisine whose hearty soups and stews, seafood dishes and spiced meats can be delicious. After many years of neglect, it has recently experienced something of a renaissance and nowadays restaurants offering *Cuina Mallorquína* are comparatively commonplace and should not be missed. Similarly appealing are the island's pastry shops (pastisserias), where you'll find the sweetest of confections.

▲ Botifarra

The islanders are extremely partial to spicy blood sausages (*botifarra*).

P.176 ▶ LANGUAGE

▲ Frito mallorquín

Pigs' offal, potatoes and onions cooked with oil; not for the faint-hearted.

P.179 ▶ LANGUAGE

▲ Ensaimada

The island's gastronomic pride and joy is the spiralled flaky pastry known as an *ensaimada*.

P.179 ▸ LANGUAGE

▶ Pa amb oli

An island favourite comprising bread rubbed with olive oil and eaten with ham, cheese or fruit.

P.178 ▸ LANGUAGE

▼ Seafood

Fish (*peix*) and shellfish (*marisc*) are a Mallorcan speciality – from cod through to octopus.

P.179 ▸ LANGUAGE

The Mallorcan Primitives

The "Mallorcan Primitives" were a school of painters that flourished on the island in the fourteenth and fifteenth centuries. Their output was entirely religious in subject, strikingly naive devotional paintings worked in bold colours on wooden panels. Examples of most of the leading artists of the school are displayed in Palma at the Museu de Mallorca, the Cathedral and the Museu Diocesà.

▲ **Francesc Comes (1379–1415)**

Comes is noted for his subtle skin textures; this painting is in Palma's church of Santa Eulalia.

P.60 ▸ PALMA

▲ Master of Montesión

This unidentified artist looked to his Catalan contemporaries for his sense of movement and tight draughtsmanship – as per this painting displayed in Palma Cathedral.

P.51 ▶ PALMA

▼ Master of the Privileges

In Palma Cathedral, this *Life of Sant Eulalia* illustrates the suffering of the eponymous saint in ecstatic detail.

P.51 ▶ PALMA

▼ Joan Desi

Desi's *Panel of La Almoina* in Palma Cathedral shows St Francis at the side of Christ.

P.51 ▶ PALMA

Beaches

For all its diverse charms, the main island activity – or lack of it – is sun-bathing on the beach. The finest sandy beaches are in the north fringing Port d'Alcúdia and Port de Pollença, on the east coast and, most fashionably – or skimpily – at the Platja de Palma outside Palma. Meanwhile, the rockier and much wilder northwest coast is home to a string of cove beaches, almost invariably of shingle and pebble.

▲ Port d'Alcúdia

Honest, there ain't no crocodiles here – and the safe and sandy beach gently shelves into the ocean.

P.121 ▶ NORTHERN MALLORCA

▲ Cala Deià, Deià

Sand is in short supply here, but the rugged mountain setting on the northwest coast is handsome compensation.

P.95 ▶ WESTERN MALLORCA

▶ Platja de Palma

Bronzed and oiled bodies throng this popular beach with a bit of verbal foreplay here and a lot of ogling there.

P.76 ▶ BAY OF PALMA

▼ Mondragó

Now safely ensconced within a nature conservation area, Mondragó's exquisite beach has escaped crass development.

P.144 ▶ SOUTHERN MALLORCA

▲ Cala Estellencs, Estellencs

This rocky cove beach enjoys a dramatic mountain setting on the northwest coast.

P.101 ▶ WESTERN MALLORCA

▼ Port de Pollença

Delightful, family-friendly beach just metres from the resort's best hotels and restaurants.

P.117 ▶ NORTHERN MALLORCA

Town and city hotels

Ten years ago, there were hardly any hotels inland from the coast – even a popular little town like Pollença had only one or two. Things are very different now with almost all of Mallorca's larger settlements, and especially Palma, equipped with a hatful of hotels, oftentimes in immaculately renovated old stone houses, which were formerly the homes of the island's landed gentry.

▲ Hotel-residencia Born, Palma

Traditional, even old-fashioned hotel set in a rambling old townhouse with an attractive, leafy courtyard.

P.68 ▶ PALMA

▼ Scott's Binissalem, Binissalem

One of the classiest hotels around, with each room kitted out in immaculate taste and style.

P.105 ▸ WESTERN MALLORCA

▲ Hotel El Guía, Sóller

Unassuming but full of character, this long-established hotel is metres from Sóller train station.

P.104 ▸ WESTERN MALLORCA

▼ Hotel Portixol, Es Portixol

Urbane boutique hotel sporting all sorts of fancy designer details; 2km east of Palma Cathedral.

P.83 ▸ BAY OF PALMA

▲ Hotel Dalt Murada, Palma

Family-run hotel in a splendid old mansion where the large and well-appointed guest rooms are kitted out with all manner of antiques.

P.68 ▸ PALMA

Rural and resort hotels

The burgeoning demand for rustic holidays has spawned several dozen country hotels, mostly located in or near the mountainous northwest coast. Some are solitary affairs, surrounded by olive and almond groves; others are in little villages and most occupy tastefully renovated old farm and merchants' houses. These rural hotels are, however, small beer compared to the superabundance of resort hotels, which range from humble little places to mammoth tower blocks with a number of delightful hotels in between.

▲ Es Molí, Deià

Superb, genteel hotel that offers the very best of food and hospitality.

P.104 ▶ WESTERN MALLORCA

▲ Can Llenaire, Port de Pollença

This handsome old manor house has been turned into a splendid hotel.

P.124 ▶ NORTHERN MALLORCA

▲ Hotel Ca's Xorc, near Sóller

Charming hotel in a creatively revamped old olive mill set among the mountains outside Sóller.

P.103 ▶ WESTERN MALLORCA

▲ Petit Hotel, Fornalutx

Atrractive, family-run hotel in a charming little village.

P.103 ▶ WESTERN MALLORCA

▼ Hotel Costa d'Or, near Deià

The *Costa d'Or* has several virtues, but its superb coastal location, high above the sea, is well-nigh unbeatable.

P.103 ▶ WESTERN MALLORCA

Mallorcan wine

In the 1990s, a concerted effort was made to raise the quality of Mallorcan wine. The results have been tremendously successful and Mallorca has now been granted two Denominació d'Origen (DO) credentials – DO wines, with their quality guarantees, being the best in Spain. One Mallorcan DO is Binissalem, named after a small, wine-producing town near Palma; the other is Pla i Llevant, which refers to a much larger area in the centre of the island.

▲ José Ferrer red Binissalem

A fine local vintage, red Binissalem is a robust and aromatic wine made predominantly from the *mantonegro* grape.

P.92 ▸ WESTERN MALLORCA

▶ Festa d'es Verema, Binissalem

The Festival of the Grape Harvest is celebrated with gusto in Binissalem; don't wear your Sunday suit.

`P.92` ▸ WESTERN MALLORCA

▼ Miquel Oliver, Petra

Specialist wine shops are springing up all over the island and this shop-cum-bodega is one of the best.

`P.133` ▸ SOUTHERN MALLORCA

▲ Herederos de Ribas Binissalem Blanco

Herederos de Ribas produces Mallorca's best white wines; this version is lively and fruity.

`P.92` ▸ WESTERN MALLORCA

▼ Bodega José Ferrer, Binissalem

The José Ferrer brand denotes Mallorca's most satisfying red wines.

`P.92` ▸ WESTERN MALLORCA

Kids' Mallorca

Pedaloe–pedalling, paddling, swimming, buckets and sand are quite enough to keep most kids happy for days on end, especially as hotel (and villa) swimming pools are commonplace, but teens may want something a bit more ambitious and Mallorca's themed water parks fit the bill. Ear plugs suggested for the mature.

▲ Hidropark, Port d'Alcúdia

An honest-to-goodness water park with pools, flumes and chutes.

P.121 ▸ NORTHERN MALLORCA

▲ Aqualand, Magaluf

Enormous water park – not the revenge of the whales.

P.79 ▸ BAY OF PALMA

▶ Aqualand, S'Arenal

Everything watery – from swimming pools to chutes and flumes.

P.76 ▸ BAY OF PALMA

▼ Western Water Park, Magaluf

Idiosyncratic mix of water park and Wild West town that gives kitsch a bad name.

P.79 ▸ BAY OF PALMA

Green Mallorca

Dotted across Mallorca, a string of natural parks provide some protection to the environment and keep the developers at bay, though it's a real pity they aren't much larger. The parks are a varied bunch, ranging from wetlands and coast through to uninhabited islets, supplemented by the chunks of wilderness – or at least semi–wilderness – that make up much of the Serra de Tramuntana mountains. The island also has three noteworthy limestone cave systems with the most enjoyable being the 450m-long series of caverns that comprise the Coves d'Artà.

▲ SA Dragonera

Now protected as a nature reserve, this craggy uninhabited islet lies off Mallorca's west coast.

P.101 ▸ WESTERN MALLORCA

▲ Serra de Tramuntana

This mountain range runs the length of the island's northwest coast, providing its most memorable scenery.

P.108 ▸ WESTERN MALLORCA & NORTHERN MALLORCA

▶ Cabrera island

Now a national park, rugged Cabrera island makes a great day out, but it's the Lilford's wall lizard that steals the show – take some fruit to tempt them out.

P.147 ▸ SOUTHERN MALLORCA

▼ Gorg Blau

High up in the mountains, the Blue Gorge reservoir enjoys an especially dramatic setting.

P.108 ▸ NORTHERN MALLORCA

▼ Mondragó Parc Natural

This east-coast park is a mixed bag of wetland, farmland and scrub.

P.143 ▸ SOUTHERN MALLORCA

▲ Coves d'Artà

Fantastic stalactites and stalagmites make these limestone caverns a fascinating place to visit.

P.139 ▸ SOUTHERN MALLORCA

Outdoor pursuits

At all the larger resorts, watersports are a big deal and companies line up to hire out equipment for everything from sailing, pedalo–pedalling, jet-skiing and windsurfing through to inflatable gear for learner swimmers. Scuba-diving and snorkelling are also commonplace with the clearest diving around the islet of Illa Dragonera and off Cala Figuera. Equally popular is hiking with hundreds of hikers descending on the Serra de Tramuntana mountains in the spring and autumn.

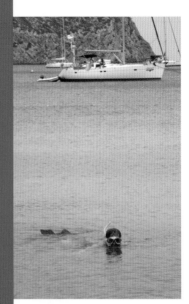

▲ Snorkelling
Snorkel away just about anywhere in Mallorca – this chap is at Port de Sóller.
P.89 ▸ WESTERN MALLORCA

▲ Jet-skiing
Jet skis can be rented at most major resorts.
P.161 ▸ ESSENTIALS

▲ Windsurfing

Windsurfing is popular at many
island resorts, especially along the
east coast.

P.161 ▸ SOUTHERN MALLORCA

▼ Bóquer valley, near Port de Pollença

The Bóquer, with its rich birdlife, makes a
perfect day's hike.

P.117 ▸ NORTHERN MALLORCA

▶ Swimming

Take the plunge into
the warm waters of the
Med; this diver is at
Mondragó.

P.144 ▸ SOUTHERN MALLORCA

Modern art in Mallorca

Mallorca has a strong, indigenous fine art tradition and has long been a favourite haunt of artists from the Spanish mainland too. Pride of artistic place goes to Joan Miró, who had his home and studio in Cala Major, but several other key galleries hold enjoyable and varied assortments of Spanish (and Mallorcan) art, notably the Palau March and the Museu d'Art Espanyol Contemporani in Palma plus the Museu Municipal Art Contemporani at Valldemossa.

▲ Es Baluard, Palma

A contemporary art museum set in an imposing bastion, which was formerly part of the city wall.

P.63 ▶ PALMA

▼ Museu Municipal d'Art Contemporani, Valldemossa monastery

The modern Spanish artist Juli Ramis (1909–90) is well-represented here; this canvas is *Dama Blava* (Blue Lady).

P.98 ▸ WESTERN MALLORCA

▼ Museu d'Art Espanyol Contemporani, Palma

This excellent museum, funded by the Juan March Foundation, explores the Spanish contribution to modern art.

P.66 ▸ PALMA

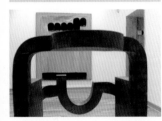

▲ Joan Miró Fundació, Cala Major

The former studio of Joan Miró has been left pretty much unchanged since the artist's death in 1983.

P.77 ▸ BAY OF PALMA

▼ Palau March Museu, Palma

Former mansion, now an enjoyable art museum, whose courtyard features Xavier Corbero's *Orgue del Mar* (Sea Organ).

P.56 ▸ PALMA

Places

Palma

Palma is a go-ahead and cosmopolitan commercial hub of over 300,000 people. As a major port of call between Europe and North Africa, the city boomed under both Moorish and medieval Christian control, but its wealth and prominence came to a sudden end with the Spanish exploitation of the New World: from the early sixteenth century, Madrid looked west across the Atlantic and Palma slipped into Mediterranean obscurity. With its appointment as the capital of the newly established autonomous region of the Balearics in 1983, the city began to discard its dusty provincialism and the new-found self-confidence is now plain to see. Today, the centre presents a splendid ensemble of lively shopping areas and refurbished old buildings, mazy lanes, fountains, gardens and sculpture, all enclosed by what remains of the old city walls and their replacement boulevards. Yet, for most visitors, Palma's main appeal is its sheer vitality: at night scores of excellent restaurants offer the best of Spanish, Catalan and Mallorcan cuisine, while the city's cafés buzz with chatter.

The Cathedral

April, May & Oct Mon–Fri 10am–5.15pm, Sat 10am–2.15pm; June–Sept Mon–Fri 10am–6.15pm, Sat 10am–2.15pm; Nov–March Mon–Fri 10am–3.15pm, Sat 10am–2.15pm; €4.50. Legend has it that when the invasion force of Jaume I of Aragón and Catalunya stood off Mallorca in 1229, a fierce gale threatened to sink the fleet. The desperate king promised to build a church dedicated to the Virgin Mary if the expedition against the Moors, who then ruled Mallorca, was successful.

▲ PALMA CATHEDRAL

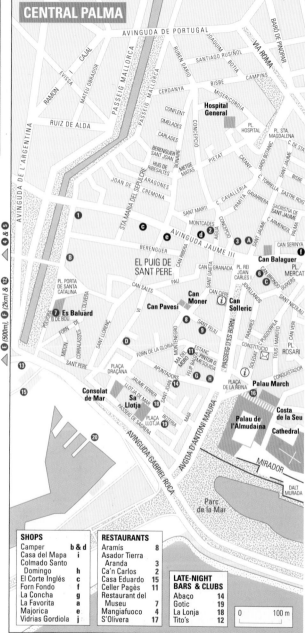

CENTRAL PALMA

SHOPS	
Camper	**b & d**
Casa del Mapa	**i**
Colmado Santo Domingo	**h**
El Corte Inglés	**c**
Forn Fondo	**f**
La Concha	**g**
La Favorita	**a**
Majorica	**e**
Vidrias Gordiola	**j**

RESTAURANTS	
Aramís	8
Asador Tierra Aranda	3
Ca'n Carlos	2
Casa Eduardo	15
Celler Pagès	11
Restaurant del Museu	7
Mangiafuoco	4
S'Olivera	17

LATE-NIGHT BARS & CLUBS	
Abaco	14
Gotic	19
La Lonja	18
Tito's	12

0   100 m

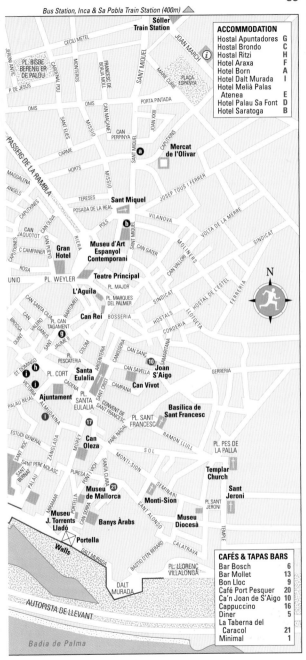

Bus Station, Inca & Sa Pobla Train Station (400m)

PLACES

ACCOMMODATION

Hostal Apuntadores	G
Hostal Brondo	C
Hostal Ritzi	H
Hotel Araxa	F
Hotel Born	A
Hotel Dalt Murada	I
Hotel Melià Palas Atenea	E
Hotel Palau Sa Font	D
Hotel Saratoga	B

CAFÉS & TAPAS BARS

Bar Bosch	6
Bar Mollet	13
Bon Lloc	9
Café Port Pesquer	20
Ca'n Joan de S'Aigo	10
Cappuccino	16
Diner	5
La Taberna del Caracol	21
Minimal	1

Orientation, city transport and information

Almost everything of interest in Palma is located in the city centre, a roughly circular affair whose southern perimeter is largely defined by the Cathedral and the remains of the old city walls, which in turn abut the coastal motorway and the harbour. The city centre's landward limits are determined by a zigzag of wide boulevards built beside or in place of the old town walls – Avinguda de la Argentina and Avinguda Gabriel Alomar i Villalonga connect with the coastal motorway, thereby completing the circle. The Via Cintura, the ring road around the suburbs, loops off from the coastal motorway to create a much larger, outer circle. The city centre itself is crossed by four interconnected avenues: Passeig d'es Born, Avinguda Jaume III, c/Unió (which becomes c/Riera at its eastern end) and Passeig de la Rambla. Your best bet is to use these four thoroughfares to guide yourself round the centre – Palma's jigsaw-like side streets and squares can be very confusing. Central Palma is about 2km in diameter, roughly thirty minutes' walk from one side to the other.

To reach the city's outskirts, take **the bus**. City buses are operated by **EMT** (Empresa Municipal de Transports) and almost all their services, which combine to link the centre with the suburbs and the nearer tourist resorts, pass through Plaça Espanya; several of the more useful services also pass through Plaça de la Reina. Tickets are available from the driver and cost €1.10 per journey within the city limits. You can buy a carnet of ten at a discount (€7.50) from most *tabacs* (tobacconists) and some newsagents. EMT also has an enquiry telephone line in Spanish and Catalan on ☏ 971 21 44 44, or visit ⊛ www.emtpalma.es.

In Palma, there's a **provincial tourist office** just off Passeig d'es Born at Plaça de la Reina 2 (Mon–Fri 9am–8pm, Sat 9am–2.30pm; ☏ 971 712 216). The main **municipal office** is on the north side of Plaça Espanya (daily 9am–8pm, ⊛ www.a-palma.es) and there's another, much smaller municipal office inside Can Solleric, at Passeig d'es Born 27 (Mon–Fri 9am–8pm, Sat 9am–1.30pm) which has limited information. The first two provide city- and island-wide information, dispensing free maps, accommodation lists, bus schedules, ferry timetables, lists of car rental firms and all sorts of special-interest leaflets, including the useful *Palma: Best Mediterranean Shopping* brochure, which details many of the city's most distinctive shops.

It was, and Jaume fulfilled his promise, starting construction work the next year. The king had a political point to make too – he built his **Cathedral** (Sa Seu in Catalan) bang on top of the Great Mosque, inside the old Moorish citadel. As it turned out, the Cathedral was five hundred years in the making, and there are architectural styles from several different eras. However, the church remains essentially Gothic, with massive exterior buttresses – its most distinctive feature – taking the weight off the pillars within.

The whole structure derives its effect from sheer height, impressive from any angle, but startling when viewed from the waterside esplanade.

The majestic proportions of its interior are seen to best advantage from the western end, from the **Portal Major** (doorway). In the central **nave**, fourteen beautifully aligned, pencil-thin pillars rise to 21m before their ribs branch out, like fronded palm trees, to support the single-span, vaulted roof. The nave, at 44m high, is one of the tallest Gothic structures in Europe, and its 121m length is of matching grandeur. Kaleidoscopic floods of light filter in through the stained-glass windows, many of which have recently been unbricked or refurbished to their former glory.

The aisles on either side of the central nave are flanked by a long sequence of **chapels**, dull affairs for the most part, dominated by dusty Baroque altars of little artistic merit. The exception, and the cathedral's one outstanding example of the Baroque, is the **Capella de Corpus Christi**, at the head of the aisle to the left of the high altar. Just across from the chapel is a massive stone pulpit from 1531 that was moved here supposedly temporarily by the Catalan architect Antoni Gaudí when he was working on the cathedral's restoration between 1904 and 1914. The pulpit is an excellent illustration of the Plateresque style with intricate floral patterns and bustling biblical scenes covering a clumsy structure, the upper portion of which is carried by telamons, male counterparts of the more usual caryatids.

The Museu de la Catedral

Same times and ticket as the Cathedral. The suite of three rooms that makes up the enjoyable **Museu de la Catedral** holds an eclectic mixture of ecclesiastical treasures. The first room's most valuable exhibit, in the glass case in the middle, is a gilded silver monstrance of extraordinary delicacy, dating from the late sixteenth century. On display around the walls are assorted chalices and reliquaries and a real curiosity, the portable altar of Jaume I, a wood and silver chessboard with each square

containing a bag of relics. The second room is mainly devoted to the Gothic works of the **Mallorcan Primitives**, a school of painters which flourished on the island in the fourteenth and fifteenth centuries, producing strikingly naive devotional works in bold colours.

The third and final room, the Baroque chapterhouse, is entered through a playfully ornate doorway, above which a delicate Madonna is overwhelmed by lively cherubic angels. Inside, pride of place goes to the High Baroque altar surmounted by the Sacred Heart, a gory representation of the heart of Jesus that was very much in vogue during the eighteenth century. Some imagination went into the designation of the reliquaries displayed round the room: there's a piece of the flogging post, three thorns from Christ's crown and even a piece of the gall-and-vinegared sponge that was offered to Jesus on the cross.

The Palau de l'Almudaina

April–Sept Mon–Fri 10am–5.45pm, Sat 10am–1pm; Oct–March Mon–Fri 10am–1pm & 4–5pm, Sat 10am–1pm; €3.20, plus €0.80 for audioguide; free entry on Wed to EU citizens showing their passport. Opposite the cathedral entrance stands

▼ PALAU DE L'ALMUDAINA

the **Palau de l'Almudaina**, originally the palace of the Moorish *wali*s (governors), and later of the Mallorcan kings. The present structure, built around a central courtyard, owes much of its appearance to Jaume II (1276–1311), who spent the last twelve years of his life in residence here. Jaume converted the old fortress into a lavish palace that incorporated both Gothic and Moorish features – and these can be observed on the self-guided tour. A particular highlight is the Arab baths, a rare survivor from Moorish times, comprising three stone-vaulted chambers.

Palau March Museu

c/Palau Reial 18 ⓦ www.fundbmarch .es. April–Oct Mon–Fri 10am–6pm, Sat 10am–2pm; Nov–March Mon–Fri 10am–5pm, Sat 10am–2pm; €3.60. The **Palau March** is an extravagant affair, whose arcaded galleries, chunky columns and large stone blocks fill out the entire block between c/Palau Reial and c/Conquistador. They were

▼ PALAU MARCH MUSEU

erected in the 1930s in the general style of the city's earlier Renaissance mansions on behalf of the Mallorcan magnate and art collector Joan March (1880–1962). He became the wealthiest man in Franco's Spain by skilfully reinvesting the profits he made from his control of the government monopoly in tobacco – though his enemies always insisted that it was smuggling that really made him rich. Much of the palace has been turned into a museum, the highlight of which is the splendid Italianate courtyard, which is used to display a potpourri of modern art drawn from the March collection. Amongst the twenty or so pieces on display, there are two Henry Moore sculptures, a Rodin torso and a fetchingly eccentric *Orgue del Mar* (Organ of the Sea) by Xavier Corbero.

The city walls and the Parc de la Mar

A flight of steps leads down from between the cathedral and the Palau de l'Almudaina to a handsomely restored section of the Renaissance **city walls**, whose mighty zigzag of bastions, bridges, gates and dry moats once encased the whole city. Earlier fortifications, constructed of sandstone blocks and adobe, had depended for their efficacy on height but, by the middle of the fifteenth century, the military balance had shifted in favour of offence, with cannons now able to breach medieval city walls with comparative ease. Walls were rebuilt much lower and thicker to absorb cannon shot, while four-faced bastions – equipped with artillery platforms – projected from the line of the walls. The whole was protected by a water-filled

▲ CITY WALLS

moat with deep, sheer sides. The Habsburgs ordered work to start on the new design of Palma's fortifications in the 1560s, though the chain of bastions was only completed in 1801.

From the foot of the steps below the cathedral, a wide and pleasant **walkway** travels along the top of the walls, providing fine views of the cathedral and an insight into the tremendous strength of the fortifications. Heading west, the walkway leads to the tiered gardens of a small Moorish-style park, which tumble down to the foot of Avinguda d'Antoni Maura, an extension of the tree-lined Passeig d'es Born (see p.63). In the opposite direction – east from the steps below the cathedral – the walkway passes above the planted palm trees, concrete terraces and ornamental lagoon of the **Parc de la Mar**, an imaginative and popular redevelopment of the disused land that once lay between the walls and the coastal motorway.

Wall and walkway zigzag along the south side of old Palma before fizzling out at Plaça Llorenç Villalonga, but long before then – after just a couple of minutes – you reach the wide stone ramp (beginning at the foot of c/Miramar) that leads down to the double **Portella gateway**, at the bottom of c/Portella.

The Banys Àrabs

c/Can Serra 7. Daily: June–Sept 9am–8pm; Oct–May 9am–6pm; €1.50. North of the Portella gate, take the first turning right for the **Banys Àrabs** (Arab Baths), one of the few genuine

▼ PORTELLA GATEWAY

▲ THE BANYS ARABS

reminders of the Moorish presence, albeit rather modest. This tenth-century brick *hammam* (bathhouse) consists of a small horseshoe-arched and domed chamber which was once heated through the floor. The arches rest on stone pillars, an irregular bunch thought to have been looted from the remains of the island's Roman buildings. The baths are reasonably well preserved, but if you've visited those in the Palau de l'Almudaina (see p.56), these are anticlimactic.

Casa Museu J. Torrents Lladó

c/Portella 9. Mid-Sept to mid-June Tues–Fri 10am–6pm, Sat 10am–2pm; mid-June to mid-Sept Tues–Fri 11am–7pm, Sat 10am–2pm; €3. The old house and studio of the Catalan artist J. Torrents Lladó (1946–93) has been pleasantly converted into a small museum, celebrating his life and work. Lladó trained in Barcelona, but he rejected Modernism in the late 1960s, moving to Mallorca in 1968. He became well known as a society portraitist, painting pictures of the rich and famous in a dark and broody Baroque style, examples of which are exhibited here along with a number of landscapes, both watercolours and sticky oils.

The Museu de Mallorca

c/Portella 5. Tues–Sat 10am–7pm, Sun 10am–2pm; €3. The **Museu de Mallorca** occupies Can Aiamans, a rambling Renaissance mansion whose high-ceilinged rooms make a delightful setting for an enjoyable medley of Mallorcan artefacts. The earliest dates from prehistoric times, fleshed out by a superb assortment of Gothic paintings and some exquisite examples of *Modernista* fittings and furnishings – though note that the (multilingual) labelling is more than a tad patchy. The collection begins in the basement, behind and to the right of the entrance, with a large and impressive section devoted to prehistoric Mallorca. There are all sorts of archeological bits and pieces here, from vases to funerary objects, and there's also an ambitious attempt to examine some of the controversies surrounding the findings. The prehistoric section leads into Roman Mallorca, whose most noteworthy relic is a battered mosaic. Then it's on to the Arab and Moorish section, which holds an exquisite selection of jewellery as well as inscribed Arab funerary tablets and some beautiful, highly decorated wooden panelling representative of Mudéjar artistry.

Retracing your steps, cross the courtyard and climb the stairs for the first of a couple of rooms devoted to the **Mallorcan Primitive painters**. On display in the first room are works by the Masters of Bishop Galiana, Montesión and Castellitx and, best of the lot, a panel painting entitled *Santa Quiteria*, whose lifelike, precisely executed figures – right down to the king's wispy beard – are typical of the gifted Master of the Privileges. Beyond, after a room full of religious statues and carved capitals, the second room of Gothic paintings is distinguished by a sequence of works by Francesc Comes (1379–1415), whose skill in catching subtle skin textures matches his Flemish contemporaries and represents a softening of the early Mallorcan Primitives' crudeness. In his striking *St George*, the saint – girl-like, with typically full lips – impales a lime-green dragon with more horns than could possibly be useful. One of the last talented exponents of Mallorcan Gothic, the Master of the Predellas – probably a certain Joan Rosató – is represented by his Bosch-like *Life of Santa Margalida*, each crowd of onlookers a sea of ugly, deformed faces and merciless eyes.

The ensuing rooms display the stodgy art of the Counter-Reformation, but the museum's top floor holds an engaging assortment of nineteenth- and early twentieth-century paintings by foreign artists once resident in Mallorca. Also on this floor are two room of **Modernista** fittings and furnishings, mostly retrieved from shops and houses that have since been demolished. Of particular interest are the charming wall tiles manufactured at the island's La Roqueta works. The pottery was in production for just twenty years (1897–1918), but this coincided with the vogue for the *Modernista* pieces in which La Roqueta excelled.

Can Oleza and Can Vivot

Up the hill, c/Portella leads to c/Morey where, at no. 9, you'll find **Can Oleza**, a sixteenth-century mansion with a cool and shaded courtyard embellished by a handsome balustrade and a set of Ionic columns. This is one of the finest of the city's many Renaissance mansions (see box on p.60), but like the others, it's rarely open to the public. Another excellent example is **Can Vivot**, an especially opulent early eighteenth-century mansion, whose spacious main courtyard, with its fetching columns and arches, is distinguished by an elegant gallery. It is located just

▼ COURTYARD, MUSEU DE MALLORCA

round the back of the Església de Santa Eulàlia (see below), at c/Can Savella 4.

Església de Santa Eulàlia

Plaça Santa Eulàlia. Mon–Fri 7am–12.30pm & 5.45–8.30pm, Sat 7am–1pm & 4.30–8.45pm, Sun 8am–1pm & 6.30–8.30pm; free.

Overshadowing the square at the top of c/Morey is the **Església de Santa Eulàlia**, which was built on the site of a mosque in the mid-thirteenth century. It took just 25 years to complete and consequently possesses an architectural homogeneity that's unusual for ecclesiastical Palma, though there some later tinkering. The church is typically Gothic in construction, with a yawning nave originally designed – as in the cathedral – to give the entire congregation a view of the high altar. The bricked-up windows of today keep out most of the light and spoil the effect, but suggestions that they be cleared have always been ignored. Framing the nave, the aisles accommodate twelve shallow chapels, one of which (the first on the right) sports a delightful Gothic panel painting in finely observed Flemish style. The other chapels are standard-issue Baroque, though they pale into insignificance when compared with the hourglass-shaped high altarpiece, a flashy Baroque extravagance of colossal proportions.

This holy ground witnessed one of the more disgraceful episodes of Mallorcan history. During Easter week in 1435, a rumour went round that Jewish townsfolk had enacted a blasphemous mock-up of the Crucifixion. There was no proof, but the Jews were promptly robbed of their possessions and condemned to be burnt at the stake unless they adopted Christianity. The ensuing mass baptism was held here at Santa Eulàlia.

Mansions in Palma

Most of medieval Palma was destroyed by fire, so the patrician **mansions** that characterize the old town today generally date from the reconstruction programme of the late seventeenth and early eighteenth centuries. Consequently they were built in the fashionable Renaissance style, with columns and capitals, loggias and arcades tucked away behind outside walls of plain stone three or four storeys high, and are surprisingly uniform in layout. Entry to almost all of these mansions was through a great arched gateway that gave onto a rectangular courtyard around which the house was built. Originally, the courtyard would have been cheered by exotic trees and flowering shrubs, and equipped with a fancy stone and ironwork well-head, where visitors could water their horses. From the courtyard, a stone exterior staircase led up to the main public rooms – with the servants' quarters below and the family's private apartments up above.

Very few of these mansions are open to the public, and all you'll see for the most part is the view from the gateway – the municipality has actually started to pay people to leave their big wooden gates open. Several have, however, passed into the public domain, the Can Aiamans, now the home of the Museu de Mallorca, being the prime example. Others worth making a detour to see are Can Oleza (p.59), Can Vivot (p.59) and Can Solleric (p.63). Only the last of these is open to the public.

The Basílica de Sant Francesc

Plaça Sant Francesc. Daily 9.30am–12.30pm & 3.30–6pm, but closed Sun afternoon; €1. Occupying the site of an old Moorish soap factory, the **Basílica de Sant Francesc** is a domineering pile that was built for the Franciscans towards the end of the thirteenth century. However, most of what you see today is seventeenth century – the result of a thoroughgoing reconstruction undertaken after the church was hit by lightning. The severe facade is pierced by a gigantic rose window of Plateresque intricacy and embellished by a Baroque doorway, the tympanum of which features a triumphant Virgin Mary engulfed by a wriggling mass of sculptured decoration. The strange statue in front of the doorway – of a Franciscan monk and a young Native American – celebrates the missionary work of **Juníper Serra** (see p.133), a Mallorcan priest despatched to California in 1768, who subsequently founded the cities of San Diego, Los Angeles and San Francisco.

The church's interior, approached through a neat and trim Gothic cloister, is distinguished by its monumental high altar, a gaudy Baroque affair featuring balustrades, lattice-work and clichéd figurines beneath a painted wooden statue of *St George and the Dragon*. It's heady stuff, as are the rolling scrolls and trumpeter-angel of the eighteenth-century pulpit on the wall of the nave, and the ornate Gothic-Baroque frontispiece of the organ just opposite. Close by, recessed chapels enclose the ambulatory and the first one on the left

▲ CLOISTER, BASÍLICA DE SANT FRANCESC

holds the **tomb of Ramon Llull**, whose bones were brought back to Palma after his martyrdom in Algeria in 1315. Considering the sanctity of the man's remains, it's an odd and insignificant-looking memorial, with Llull's alabaster effigy set high up on the wall to the right of the chapel altarpiece at a disconcertingly precarious angle.

Plaça Sant Jeroni

In the depths of the old town, **Plaça Sant Jeroni** is a pretty little piazza set around a diminutive water fountain. The severe stone walls of a former convent, now a college, dominate one side of the square, while the **Església de Sant Jeroni** fills out another. The church facade is mostly a plain stone wall, but it does sport two elaborate doorways, the one to the left a swirl of carved foliage and garlands of fruit. The tympanum portrays the well-known story of St Jerome in the desert, during which the saint endures all sorts of tribulations and temptations, but remains true to his faith. The interior is a seventeenth-century affair with heavy stone vaulting, though unfortunately it's rarely open to the public. The highlight here is various paintings, amongst them several works by the Mallorcan Primitives, including Pere Terrencs' lively *Sant Jeroni*.

The Museu Diocesà

c/Calders 2. Mon–Fri 10am–1pm & 4–7pm, though times may vary; €3.

The **Museu Diocesà** (Diocesan Museum) is housed in the plain nineteenth-century chapel of a former seminary just off Plaça Sant Jeroni. The premises may be uninspiring, but the museum does hold an excellent collection of **Mallorcan Primitives**, including a charming *St Paul* panel painting by the Master of Bishop Galiana, whose crisp draughtsmanship was very much in the Catalan tradition. The painting is a didactic cartoon-strip illustrating the life of St Paul, who is shown with his Bible open and sword in hand, a militant view of the church that must have accorded well with the preoccupations of the powerful bishops of Mallorca.

A second highlight is the *Passion of Christ* by an unknown artist dubbed the Master of the Passion of Mallorca. Dated to the end of the thirteenth century, the painting follows a standard format, with a series of small vignettes outlining the story of Christ, but the detail is warm and gentle: the Palm Sunday donkey leans forward pushing his nose towards a child; one of the disciples reaches out across the Last Supper table for the fish; and two of Jesus' disciples slip their sandals off in eager anticipation during the washing of the feet. By contrast, Alonso

de Sedano's sixteenth-century *Crucifixion* is a sophisticated work of strong, deep colours within a triangulated structure. Above is the blood-spattered, pale-white body of Christ, while down below – divided by the Cross – are two groups, one of hooded mourners, the other a trio of nonchalant Roman soldiers in contemporary Spanish dress. Also noteworthy is a large and dramatic *St George and the Dragon*, a panel painting of the late fifteenth century attributed to Pere Niçard with the stern fortifications of Palma in the background.

Església de Monti-Sion

c/Monti-Sion. Usually open Mon–Fri 7–8.30am. From Plaça Sant Jeroni, c/Seminari and then c/Monti-Sion run west through one of the oldest parts of the city, a jumble of old and distinguished mansions hidden behind high stone walls. On the way, you pass the **Església de Monti-Sion**, whose thundering facade is a hectic heap of angels and saints, coats of arms and wriggling foliage. Below the figure of the Virgin, look out for a strangely inconclusive representation of the Devil – half-sheep, half-dragon.

Plaça Cort

With its elegant nineteenth-century facades, bustling **Plaça Cort**, just to the west edge of the Església de Santa Eulalia, was named after the various legal bodies – both secular and religious – which were once concentrated here. Along with much of the rest of Spain, Mallorca possessed a truly Byzantine legal system until the whole caboodle was swept away and rationalized during the Napoleonic occupation. On one side, the square is dominated by the **Ajuntament** (Town Hall), a debonair example of the late Renaissance style. Pop in for a look at the grand and self-assured foyer, which mostly dates from the nineteenth century, and the six folkloric *gigantones* (giant carnival figures) stored here – four in a corner, the other two tucked against the staircase.

Passeig d'es Born and Can Solleric

Distinguished by the stone sphinxes at its top and bottom, the **Passeig d'es Born**, which runs just to the west of the cathedral, has been the city's principal promenade since the early fifteenth century, when the stream that ran here was diverted following a disastrous flash flood. Nowadays, this leafy avenue is too traffic-congested to be especially endearing, but it's still at the heart of the city, and close to some of Palma's most fashionable bars and restaurants. It's also overlooked by several of the city's most lavish mansions, notably the loggia of the Palau March – now the site of the *Cappuccino* café (see p.70).

▼ STONE SPHINX, PASSEIG D'ES BORN

– and **Can Solleric** (Tues–Sat 10am–2pm & 5–9pm, Sun 10am–1.30pm; free) at no. 27, a handsome Italianate structure of heavy wooden doors, marble columns and vaulted ceilings built for a family of cattle and olive oil merchants in 1763. Recently restored, the house now displays roving exhibitions of modern art and is the temporary home of a small tourist information desk.

Avinguda Jaume III

Avinguda Jaume III marches west from the top of Passeig d'es Born lined by the stone arcades of the sturdy shop- and office-blocks that were built in the 1940s. This is Francoista architecture at its most appealing – very symmetrical and self-consciously Spanish – and it's here you'll find some of the island's chicest clothes shops, as well as downtown's biggest department store, El Corte Inglés (see p.72). There's something very engaging about the airs and graces of the avenue, with its jostle of beshorted tourists and besuited Spaniards. The web of ancient alleys immediately to the north is another attractive corner of the city, all high stone walls and dignified old mansions focused on **c/Concepció**.

Es Baluard Museu d'art modern i contemporani

Plaça Porta Santa Catalina ⓦ www .esbaluard.org. June–Sept Tues–Sun 10am–11pm; Oct–May Tues–Sun 10am–8pm; €6. At top of the Avinguda Jaume III, the **Passeig Mallorca** is bisected by the deep, walled watercourse which once served as the city moat and is now an especially handsome feature of the city. Turn left here, on this side of the *passeig*, and you soon reach the mammoth **bastion** which long anchored the southwest corner of the Renaissance city wall and now holds the much lauded **Es Baluard Museu d'art modern i contemporani** (Museum of Modern and Contemporary Art) on Plaça Porta Santa Catalina. The museum has three floors – the top two floors for the permanent collection, the other for temporary exhibitions – subdivided into themed areas such as 'Mediterranean Landscapes' and the grandly named 'Figurative renovation during the first half of the twentieth century'. However, at the risk of sounding churlish, the most striking feature is just how few paintings there are on display and, given the lavishness of the setting, the small extent of the permanent collection. That said, there are a handful of Miró's, including one of his few attempts at landscape painting, and a rare and unusual sample of Picasso ceramics, most memorably a striking white, ochre and black vase-like piece entitled *Big Bird Corrida*. Much more successful are the large, geometric **sculptures** that have

been carefully positioned outside the museum across the top of the bastion in a perfect match of style and setting. In particular, look out for the irregular, rusting cubes of Gerardo Rueda's (1926–96) *Almagra* and the plaque-like severity of *Triplico* by José Luís Sanchez (b.1926). There are also grand views out over the coast from the bastion and an outstanding restaurant (see p.71).

Plaça Mercat and Plaça Weyler

From the top of Avinguda Jaume III, proceed east to reach tiny **Plaça Mercat**, the site of two identical *Modernista* buildings commissioned by a wealthy baker, Josep Casasayas, in 1908. Each is a masterpiece of flowing, organic lines tempered by graceful balconies and decorated with fern-leaf and butterfly motifs. Just along the street, on **Plaça Weyler**, stands a further *Modernista* extravagance, the magnificent **Gran Hotel** of 1903. Recently scrubbed and polished, the facade boasts playful arches, balconies, columns and bay windows enlivened with

▲ ES BALUARD GALLERY

▲ GRAN HOTEL, PLAÇA WEYLER

tympanum sports a fanciful relief dedicated to the nine Muses of Greek mythology. This is the city's main auditorium for classical music, ballet and opera, and it has recently reopened after a major revamp.

Plaça Major and Plaça Marquès del Palmer

On both sides of the Teatre Principal, steep flights of steps lead up to **Plaça Major**, a large pedestrianized square built on the site of the former headquarters of the Spanish Inquisition. The square, a rather formal affair with a symmetrical portico running around its perimeter, once housed the fish and vegetable market, but nowadays it's popular for its pavement cafés. On the south side of Plaça Major lies the much smaller **Plaça Marquès del Palmer**, a cramped setting for two fascinating *Modernista* edifices. The more dramatic is **Can Rei**, a five-storey apartment building splattered with polychrome ceramics and

intricate floral trimmings and brilliant polychrome ceramics inspired by Hispano-Arabic designs. The interior houses a café-bar, a good art bookshop and the spacious **Fundació La Caixa** art gallery (Tues–Sat 10am–9pm, Sun 10am–2pm; free), which organizes an excellent and wide-ranging programme of exhibitions. The permanent collection is confined to a large sample of work by the Catalan Impressionist-Expressionist Hermen Anglada-Camarasa, who is best known for the evocative Mallorcan land- and seascapes he produced during his sojourn on the island from 1914 to 1936.

There's another excellent example of *Modernismo* across the street from the Gran Hotel, in the floral motifs and gaily painted wooden doorway of the **Forn des Teatre** (theatre bakery) at Plaça Weyler 9. A few metres away looms the Neoclassical frontage of the **Teatre Principal**, whose

▼ MODERNISTA ARCHITECTURE

floral decoration, its centrepiece a gargoyle-like face set between a pair of winged dragons.

The facade of the adjacent **L'Àguila** building is of similar ilk, though there's greater emphasis on window space, reflecting its original function as a department store.

The Museu d'Art Espanyol Contemporani

c/Sant Miquel 11. Mon–Fri 10am–6.30pm, Sat 10.30am–2pm; free. On the pleasant shopping street of c/Sant Miquel, the **Banca March** occupies a fine Renaissance mansion whose *Modernista* flourishes date from a tasteful refurbishment in 1917. The building has two entrances, one to the bank, the other to the upper-floor **Museu d'Art Espanyol Contemporani**, which features changing selections from the contemporary art collection of the March family (see p.56). Dozens of works by twentieth-century Spanish artists are displayed, the intention being to survey the Spanish contribution to modern art, a theme which is further developed by temporary exhibitions. The earliest piece, Picasso's *Tête de Femme* (1907), is of particular interest, being one of the first of the artist's works to be influenced by the primitive forms that were to propel him from the re-creation of natural appearances into abstract art. Miró and Dalí are also well represented, but the bulk of the collection is remorselessly modern and, although there are some touches of humour, most of it is hard to warm to, especially the allegedly "vigorous" abstractions of both the El Paso (Millares, Saura, Feito, Canogar) and the Parpalló (Sempere, Alfaro) groupings of the late 1950s.

The harbourfront – Sa Llotja

The various marinas, shipyards, fish docks and ferry and cargo terminals that make up Palma's harbourfront extend west for several kilometres from the foot of Avinguda d'Antoni Maura. The harbour is at its prettiest at this eastern end, where a cycling and walking path skirts the seashore, with boats to one side and bars, restaurants, apartment blocks and the smart hotels of the Avinguda Gabriel Roca – often dubbed the Passeig Marítim – on the other. The first harbourfront landmark is the fifteenth-century **Sa Llotja**, the city's former stock exchange (Tues–Sat 11am–2pm & 5–9pm, Sun 11am–2pm; free). This carefully composed late Gothic building, with four octagonal turrets, slender, spiralling columns and tall windows, now hosts frequent, and occasionally excellent, exhibitions (some of which you'll have to pay to get into). Next door, the distinguished **Consolat de Mar** was built in the 1660s to accommodate the Habsburg officials who supervised maritime affairs in this part of the empire. Today, as the home of the president of the Balearic islands, it's closed to the public, but the outside is worth a second look for its pair of crusty old cannons and elegant Renaissance gallery. The forlorn-looking gate between the two buildings – the **Porta Vella del Moll** – originally stood at the bottom of Avinguda d'Antoni Maura, where it was the main entrance into the city from the sea, but was moved here when portions of the town wall were demolished in the 1870s.

▲ CASTELL DE BELLVER

The Castell de Bellver

April–Sept Mon–Sat 8.30am–8.30pm, Sun 10am–6.30pm; Oct–March Mon–Sat 8.30am–7pm, Sun 10am–5pm; €2, but free on Sun. Take bus #6 from Plaça de la Reina to Plaça Gomila, which leaves a steep 1.5km walk up the hill. If you're driving, turn off Avinguda Joan Miró (one-way west) onto the circuitous c/Camilo José Cela. Boasting superb views of Palma from a wooded hilltop some 3km west of the city centre, the **Castell de Bellver** is a handsome, strikingly well-preserved fortress built for Jaume II at the beginning of the fourteenth century. The castle's immensely thick walls and steep ditches encircle a central keep that incorporates three imposing towers. In addition, an overhead, single-span stone arch connects the keep to a massive, freestanding tower, built as a final refuge. To enhance defence, the walls curve and bend and the interconnecting footbridges are set at oblique angles to each other. It's all very impressive – and looks well-nigh impregnable – but the castle was also intended to serve as a royal retreat from the summer heat, and so the austere outside walls hide a commodious, genteel-looking circular courtyard, surrounded by two tiers of inward-facing arcades that once belonged to the residential suites. In the event, the castle's construction was all but a waste of time as improvements in artillery soon rendered it obsolete, and the stronghold didn't last long as a royal residence either. As early as the 1350s the keep was in use as a prison, a function it performed until 1915. More recently, the castle interior has been turned into a museum tracking through the history of the city, with Roman statuary the main highlight. After you've explored the castle, you can wander the unsigned **footpaths** through the pine-scented woods that surround it.

Accommodation

Hostal Apuntadores

c/Apuntadors 8 ☎971 713491, ⓦwww.palma-hostales.com. Simple, straightforward rooms in an old house with a central location just off Passeig d'es Born. Some rooms are en suite, others have shared facilities. A long-established *hostal* but light sleepers should bag a room at the back as c/Apuntadors can get very noisy at night. Breakfast is served in the café in the reception area. €45.

Hostal Brondo

c/Ca'n Brondo 1 ☎ 971 719043, ⓦ www.hostalbrondo.net. In a central but quiet street, this stylish little place occupies a sympathetically modernized old house complete with ancient stone arches and traditional whitewashed plasterwork. The guest rooms are decorated in plain but pleasant modern style and are both en suite and with shared facilities. Shared bath €45, en suite €55.

Hostal Ritzi

c/Apuntadors 6 ☎ 971 714610, ⓦ www.hostalritzi.com. Well-regarded and long-established one-star *hostal* in the centre of the city, just off Passeig d'es Born. Occupies an ancient but well-kept five-storey house and although the rooms, both en suite and with shared facilities, could hardly be described as super comfortable, they are perfectly adequate. Shared bath €45, en suite €55.

Hotel Araxa

c/Alférez Cerdá 22 ☎ 971 731640, ⓦ www.hotelaraxa.com. Attractive four-storey modern hotel with pleasant gardens and an outdoor swimming pool. Most rooms have balconies. It's in a quiet residential area about 2km west of the centre, not far from the Castell de Bellver. To get there by public transport, take EMT bus #6 and get off at c/Marquès de la Sènia, just before the start of Avgda Joan Miró; it's a five- to ten-minute walk from the bus stop. €110.

Hotel Born

c/Sant Jaume 3 ☎ 971 712942, ⓦ www.hotelborn.com. Delightful hotel in an excellent downtown location, set in a refurbished mansion with big wooden doors and a lovely courtyard, where you can have breakfast under the palm trees. The rooms, most of which face onto the courtyard, are comfortable if a little plain, and all have a/c. It's a popular spot, so book early in high season. €120.

Hotel Dalt Murada

c/Almudaina 6 ☎ 971 425300, ⓦ www.daltmurada.com. One of the most delightful hotels in the city, this family-run place occupies a splendid old mansion that comes complete with many of its eighteenth-century – and even earlier – features. Each of the guest rooms has its own character, but they are all large and extremely well appointed, and most hold antique furnishings; the exception is the immaculately modern penthouse suite. Breakfast is served in the garden, weather permitting. Great location too – down an old cobbled alley metres from Plaça Cort. The family also owns the small and much plainer, six-room **Hotel Casa Padrina**, which occupies a late nineteenth-century townhouse in somewhat gloomy surroundings at the corner of c/Missió and c/Tereses. Dalt Murada €180; Casa Padrina €120.

Hotel Melià Palas Atenea

Passeig Marítim (Avgda Gabriel Roca) 29 ☎ 971 281400, ⓦ www.solmelia.com. A vast, classy 1960s-style foyer leads to attractively furnished, comfortable rooms with balconies overlooking the bay. There's also an inviting bar. €150.

Hotel Palau Sa Font

c/Apuntadors 38 ☎ 971 712277, ⓦ www.palausafont.com. This smooth and polished four-star hotel, decorated in earthy Italian colours and graced by sculptures and other modern works of art, manages to be both stylish and welcoming. There's a small pool on the roof terrace, and some rooms enjoy inspiring views of the cathedral. Breakfast included. Discounts are frequent – though note that cards are not accepted on special deals. €155.

Hotel Saratoga

Passeig Mallorca 6 ☎ 971 727240, ⓦ www.hotelsaratoga.es. Bright, modern, centrally located hotel in a smart seven-storey block complete with a rooftop café and garden swimming pool. Rooms are neat and trim, with marble floors and balconies either overlooking the boulevard (which can be noisy) or an interior courtyard (much quieter). Substantial banquet-breakfast included. €120.

Cafés and tapas bars

Bar Bosch

Plaça Rei Joan Carles I. Daily 8am–2am. One of the most popular and inexpensive *tapas* bars in town, the traditional haunt of the city's intellectuals and usually humming with conversation. At peak times

you'll need to be assertive to get served.

Bar Mollet

c/Contramoll Mollet 2 ☎ 971 719871. Mon–Sat 6am–4.30pm. Located just across from the fish market, and with some of the freshest fish in town. The first-rate *menú del día* (Mon–Fri €10, Sat €15) includes wine and dessert.

Bon Lloc

c/Sant Feliu 7. Mon–Sat 1–4pm. One of the few vegetarian café-restaurants on the island, with good food at low prices and an informal, homely atmosphere in pleasant premises; the set menu goes for under €20.

Café Port Pesquer

Avgda Gabriel Roca s/n. Daily from 10am till late. Also known as *El Pesquero*, this bright and breezy café-restaurant, with its expansive open-air terrace, occupies a distinctly nautical, chalet-like structure right on the bay shore, overlooking the fishing jetties a couple of minutes' walk east of Avgda Argentina. Serves up a good

▼ CA'N JOAN DE S'AIGO

range of *tapas* (€7–10), a filling version of *pa amb oli* with cheese or ham (€12) and a range of fresh fish dishes for €14 and up. Note, however, that at busy times the service can be a tad tardy.

Ca'n Joan de S'Aigo

c/Can Sanç 10. Daily except Tues 8am–9pm. A long-established coffeehouse with wonderful, freshly baked *ensaimadas* (spiral pastry buns) and fruit-flavoured mousses to die for. Charming decor too, from the kitschy water fountain to the traditional Mallorcan green-tinted chandeliers. It's on a tiny alley near Plaça Santa Eulalia – take c/Sant Crist and its continuation c/Canisseria, then turn right.

Cappuccino

c/Conquistador. Daily 10am–11pm. Attractive terrace café occupying the lower part of the Palau March. The food is uninspiring, but the setting is great.

Diner

c/Sant Magí 23, Santa Catalina ☎971 736222. Open seven days a week, 24 hours a day. A little slice of Americana, serving hamburgers, milkshakes, hash browns, pancakes, BLTs and Dixie fried chicken – all homemade and using only the best ingredients. Phone for take-away.

La Taberna del Caracol

c/Sant Alonso 2 ☎971 714908. Mon–Sat 1–3.30pm & 7.30–11.30pm. Deep in the depths of the old town, this smashing *tapas* bar occupies charming old premises, all wooden beams and ancient arches. A first-rate range of *tapas* begins at just €6. Reservations advised at peak times.

Minimal

Passeig Mallorca 10. Mon–Sat 11am–11pm. Slick, modern café in a pleasant setting in the stone arcade bordering (an almost traffic-free part of) the *passeig*. Illy coffee and a delicious range of salads from €8–12.

Restaurants

Aramís

c/Montenegro 1 ☎971 725232. Mon–Fri 1–3.30pm & 8-11pm, Sat 8–11pm. Set in a sympathetically refurbished old stone mansion on a side street off Passeig d'es Born, this superb restaurant has an imaginative menu with an international range of dishes – ravioli and pumpkin, wild mushrooms en croute for example – and there's an unbeatable *menú del día* (€14) plus a wonderful house red. Reservations recommended.

Asador Tierra Aranda

c/Concepció 4 ☎971 714256. Tues–Sat 1–4pm & 8–11pm, Sun & Mon 1–4pm only; closed for annual holidays in July. A smart and fairly formal carnivore's paradise in an old mansion off Avgda Jaume III: meats either grilled over open fires or roasted in wood-fired ovens, with suckling pig and lamb house specialities. Weather permitting, you can also eat in the garden. Reservations advised.

Ca'n Carlos

c/Aigua 5 ☎971 713869. Mon–Sat 1–4pm & 8–11pm. Charming, family-run restaurant featuring first-class Mallorcan cuisine that takes in such delights as cuttlefish and snails. The menu isn't extensive, but everything is carefully prepared and there's a daily special as well as a fish of the day. Good dishes to sample are *fava parada* (dried bean stew) and *caragols de la mallorquina* (snails). Main courses average around €15.

Casa Eduardo

Contramoll Mollet 4 ☎971 716574. Tues–Sat 1–3.30pm & 8–11pm. Spick-and-span restaurant located upstairs in one of the plain modern buildings beside the fish dock. There's an enjoyable view of the harbour, but the real treat is the fresh fish – a wonderful range, all simply prepared, though grilled is best. It's located just across from – and east of – the foot of Avgda Argentina. Main courses average €16.

Celler Pagès

c/Felip Bauza 2, off c/Apuntadors ☎971 726036. Mon–Sat 1–3.30pm & 8–11pm. Tiny, inexpensive restaurant with an easy-going family atmosphere serving traditional Mallorcan food – try the stuffed marrows with home-made mayonnaise on the side, while the roast leg of duck with dried plums and grilled vegetables is delicious. Reserve at weekends.

Mangiafuoco

Plaça Vapor 4, Santa Catalina ☎971 451072. Daily except Tues 1.30–3.30pm & 8–11pm. Tuscan-owned restaurant-cum-wine bar offering top-notch Italian food and specializing in dishes featuring truffles, which are flown in weekly from Tuscany. Try the *pappardelle al tartuffo* and prepare to be wowed, especially when it's washed down with one of the superb house wines. Attractive setting, too – metres from the top of the low ridge that overlooks the harbourfront.

Restaurant del Museu

Es Baluard Museu, Plaça Porta Santa Catalina s/n ☎971 908199. Tues–Sun noon–3.30pm & 8–11pm. Adjacent to the Es Baluard gallery (see p.63), this excellent restaurant occupies two modernist glass cubes with views out across the bay. The menu is based on Mallorcan cuisine, but there are all sorts of international flourishes – try the lamb. Main courses cost around €16 in the evening, slightly less during the day.

S'Olivera

c/Morey 5 ☎971 729581. Mon–Sat 1.30–3.30pm & 8–11pm. Appealing restaurant, with antique bric-a-brac and paintings dotted round the walls. Food includes a first-rate range of *tapas* (around €6 per portion), plus quality Spanish cuisine and a good-value lunchtime *menú del día* (€10).

Late-night bars and clubs

Abaco

c/Sant Joan 1 ☎971 714939. Daily 9pm–2am, but closed for most of Jan. Set in a charming old mansion, this is easily Palma's most unusual bar, with an interior straight out of a Busby Berkeley musical: fruits cascading down its stairway, caged birds hidden amid patio foliage, elegant music and a daily flower bill you could live on for a month. Drinks, as you might imagine, are extremely expensive (cocktails cost as much as €15) but you're never hurried into buying one. It is, however, rather too sedate to be much fun if you're on the razzle. Located in the city centre, just off c/Apuntadors.

Gotic

Plaça Llotja 2. Tiny bar and café with a candlelit patio and pavement tables that nudge out across the square, adding a touch of romance.

La Lonja

c/Llotja de Mar 2. A popular, well-established haunt, with revolving doors and pleasantly old-fashioned decor; the background music caters for (almost) all tastes. There's *tapas* as well, and you can sit out in the square right in front of Sa Llotja.

Tito's

Plaça Gomila 3 ℡ 971 730017, ⓦ www.titosmallorca.com. June to early Sept daily 11pm–5am, Oct–May Fri–Sun 11pm–5am. With its stainless-steel and glass exterior, this long-established nightspot looks a bit like something from a sci-fi film. Outdoor lifts carry you up from Avgda Gabriel Roca (the back entrance) to the dance floor, which pulls in huge crowds from many countries – or you can go in through the front entrance on Plaça Gomila. The music (anything from house to mainstream pop) lacks conviction, but it's certainly loud. The Avgda Gabriel Roca entrance is just on the city centre side of the Jardins La Quarentena gardens. Admission about €20.

Shopping

Camper

Avgda Jaume III 16 & Sant Miquel 17. Mon–Sat 10am–8.30pm. Love them or hate them, Camper shoes are extraordinarily popular and they are made in Mallorca. This outlet sells the range.

Casa del Mapa

c/Sant Domingo 11. Mon–Fri 10am–1.30pm & 5–7.30pm, Sat 10am–1pm. Good driving and walking maps of Mallorca can be surprisingly hard to get hold of, but this specialist map shop – the only one on the island – rectifies matters.

Colmado Santo Domingo

c/Sant Domingo 1. Mon–Fri 10am–1.30pm & 5–7.30pm, Sat 10am–1pm. A tiny, cave-like, old-fashioned store packed with hanging sausages and local fruit and veg; it's right in the centre, metres from Plaça Cort. The sausages you should try carry the "Sobrasada de Mallorca de Cerdo Negro" label, which guarantees they are made from the island's own indigenous black pig.

El Corte Inglés

Avgda Jaume III 15. Mon–Sat 9.30am–9.30pm. The biggest and best department store in the city centre, which – as you might expect – sells just about everything. Has a substantial food and drink section in its basement, where you can track down lots of Mallorcan wines.

Forn Fondo

c/Unió 15. Mon–Sat 8am–8.30pm & Sun 8am–2pm. Palma has lots of good cake and pastry shops (*pastelerías*) and this is one of the best. An excellent second option is **Forn des Teatre**, just along the street at Plaça Weyler 9 (Mon–Sat 9am–12.30pm & 4.30–7.30pm).

La Concha

c/Jaume II 19. Mon–Fri 10am–1.30pm & 5–8pm, Sat 9.30am–1pm. Old-fashioned shop which stocks cheap and cheerful **souvenirs** such as brightly

▲ CHANDELIER, VIDRIAS GORDIOLA

coloured Spanish fans, garish Spanish plates, model cherubs and mini-*gigantones* (carnival figures). Also sells **siurells**, white clay whistles flecked with red and green paint and shaped to depict a figure, an animal or a scene (a man sitting on a donkey, for instance); *siurells* have been given as tokens of friendship in Mallorca for hundreds of years.

La Favorita
c/Sant Miquel 38. Mon–Fri 9.30am– 1.30pm & 5–7.30pm, Sat 10am–1pm. One of the city's best delis with all sorts of Spanish and Italian treats and a superb range of oils.

Majorica
Avgda Jaume III 11. Mon–Fri 9.30am–1.30pm & 4.30–8pm, Sat 9.30am–1.30pm. The official outlet for the main manufacturer of Mallorca's well-known artificial pearls. Made from glass globules painted with many layers of a glutinous liquid primarily composed of fish scales, the industry is based in Manacor, in the heart of the island.

Vidrias Gordiola
c/Victòria 2. Mon–Fri 10am–1.30pm & 4.30–8pm, Sat 10am–1.30pm. Glass-making is a traditional island craft and this shop, an outlet for the main Mallorcan manufacturer, has a fine range of clear and tinted glassware, from bowls, vases and lanterns through to some wonderfully intricate chandeliers.

The Bay of Palma

Arched around the sheltered waters of the Bay of Palma (Badia de Palma) are the package-tourist resorts of sun, sex and booze folklore. This thirty-kilometre-long stretch of coastline is divided into a score or more resorts and, although it's often difficult to fathom where one ends and another begins, each has evolved its own identity, in terms either of the nationalities they attract, the income group they appeal to or the age range they cater for.

East of Palma lies S'Arenal, mainly geared up for young Germans, with dozens of pounding bars and all-night clubs as well as one of Mallorca's best beaches, the Platja de Palma. West of Palma, the coast bubbles up into the low, rocky hills and sharp coves that prefigure the mountains further west. The sandy beaches here are far smaller but the terrain makes the tourist development seem less oppressive. Cala Major, the first stop, was once the playground of the super rich. It has hit grittier

times, but some of the grand old buildings have survived, and the Fundació Pilar i Joan Miró makes a fascinating detour. The neighbouring resort of Illetes is a good deal more polished, boasting comfortable hotels and attractive cove beaches, while, moving west again, Portals Nous has an affluent and exclusive marina. Next comes British-dominated Palma Nova, a major package-holiday destination popular with all ages, and adjacent Magaluf, where high-rise hotels, thumping

Getting around

Buses along the Badia de Palma coast are fast and efficient. The resorts in the immediate vicinity of Palma are served by **EMT** (Spanish and Catalan information line ☎971 214444, ⊛www.emtpalma.es), all of whose buses pass through Palma's Plaça Espanya; most EMT buses also have several other city-centre stops. Principal EMT services include bus #3, heading west to Cala Major & Illetes; bus #15 running through Ca'n Pastilla to S'Arenal; and bus #17, which travels the old coastal road east through Es Portixol to Ca'n Pastilla. Further afield, the remaining Badia de Palma resorts, including Portals Nous, Magaluf and Peguera, plus the likes of Port Andratx (see p.102) and Sant Elm (see p.101), are served by **TransaBús** (Spanish/Catalan information line ☎971 177777, ⊛http://tib.caib .es); all TransaBús services leave from the bus station on c/Eusebi Estada. **Ticket prices** are incredibly low – the twenty-five-minute journey to S'Arenal, for instance, costs just €1.15.

Driving is straightforward: the *autopista* (motorway) shoots along the coast from S'Arenal right round to Palma Nova and then slices across a narrow peninsula to reach Santa Ponça and Peguera. Alternatively, you can choose to take the old coastal road through most of the resorts, heading east from Palma to Es Portixol and ultimately S'Arenal, or west from Cala Major to Magaluf.

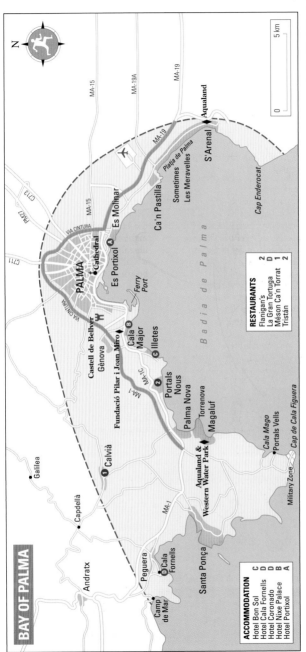

BAY OF PALMA

RESTAURANTS
Flanigan's 2
La Gran Tortuga D
Mesón Ca'n Torrat 1
Tristán 2

ACCOMMODATION
Hotel Bon Sol C
Hotel Cala Fornells D
Hotel Coronado D
Hotel Nixe Palace B
Hotel Portixol A

nightlife and a substantial sandy beach cater to a youthful and very British crowd. South of Magaluf, the charming cove beach of Portals Vells is a real surprise, sheltered by an undeveloped, pine-studded peninsula. West of Magaluf, the coastal highway leaves the Badia de Palma for unpretentious Santa Ponça before pushing on to Peguera, a large, sprawling family resort with attractive sandy beaches. Next door – and much more endearing – is tiny Cala Fornells, where pretty villas thread along the coastal hills. From here, it's another short hop to the pleasant bay that encloses the burgeoning resort of Camp de Mar.

The Platja de Palma

The **Platja de Palma**, the four-kilometre stretch of sandy beach that defines the four coterminous (and indistinguishable) resorts of Ca'n Pastilla, Sometimes, Les

▼ PLATJA DE PALMA

Meravelles and S'Arenal, is crowded with serious sun-seekers, a sweating throng of bronzed and oiled bodies slowly roasting in the heat. The beach is also a busy pick-up place, the spot for a touch of verbal foreplay before the night-time bingeing begins. It is, as they say, fine if you like that sort of thing – though older visitors look rather marooned. A wide and pleasant walkway lined with palm trees runs behind the beach and this, in turn, is edged by a long sequence of bars, restaurants and souvenir shops. A toy-town tourist "train" shuttles up and down the walkway, but there's so little to distinguish one part of the beach from another that it's easy to become disoriented. To maintain your bearings, keep an eye out for the series of smart, stainless-steel beach bars, each numbered and labelled, in Castilian, *balneario*, strung along the shore: *Balneario* no. 15 is by the Ca'n Pastilla marina, while no. 1 is near S'Arenal harbour.

Singling out any part of this massive complex is a pretty pointless exercise, but the area around S'Arenal harbour does at least have a concentration of facilities. There's car rental, currency exchange, boat trips and nightclubs as well as a couple of above-average places to eat.

Aqualand

Palma–S'Arenal road, km 15. May–June & Sept–Oct daily 10am– 5pm; July–Aug daily 10am–6pm; ⓦwww.aqualand.es; €21. Between the *autopista* and the eastern edge of the resort, about 15km east of Palma lies Aqualand, a huge leisure complex of swimming pools, water flumes and kiddies' playgrounds.

▲ FUNDACIÓ PILAR I JOAN MIRÓ

Cala Major

Crowded **Cala Major** snakes along a hilly stretch of coastline a kilometre or two to the west of Palma's ferry port. Overlooking the main street (which comprises a section of the MA-1C coast road), occasional *Modernista* mansions and the luxurious *Nixe* hotel are reminders of halcyon days when the resort was a byword for elegance. The king of Spain still runs a palace here – the Palacio de Marivent, on the main street close to the *autopista* at the east end of the resort.

The Fundació Pilar i Joan Miró

c/Joan de Saridakis 29, Cala Major. Mid-May to mid-Sept Tues–Sat 10am–7pm, Sun 10am–3pm; mid-Sept to mid-May Tues–Sat 10am–6pm, Sun 10am–3pm; ⓦ miro.palmademallorca .es. €5. EMT bus #3. Opposite the Palacio de Marivent in Cala Major, the signposted turning to Gènova leads up the hill for 500m to the Fundació Pilar i Joan Miró, where the painter Joan Miró lived and worked for much of the 1950s, 1960s and 1970s. Initially – from 1920 – the young Miró was involved with the Surrealists in Paris and contributed to all their major exhibitions: his wild squiggles, supercharged with bright colours, prompted André Breton, the leading theorist of the movement, to describe Miró as "the most Surrealist of us all". In the 1930s he adopted a simpler style, abandoning the decorative complexity of his earlier work for a more minimalist use of symbols, though the highly coloured forms remained. Miró returned to Barcelona, the city of his birth, in 1940, where he continued to work in the Surrealist tradition, though as an avowed opponent of Franco his position was uneasy. In 1957, he moved to Mallorca, its relative isolation offering a degree of safety. His wife and mother were both Mallorcan, which must have influenced his decision, as did the chance to work in his own purpose-built studio with its view of the coast. Even from the relative isolation of Franco's Spain he remained an influential figure, prepared to experiment with all kinds of media, right up until his death here in Cala Major in 1983.

The expansive hillside premises of the Fundació include Miró's old studio, an unassuming affair with views over the bay that has been left pretty much as it was at the time of his death. It's worth a quick gander for a flavour of how the man worked – tackling a dozen or so canvases at the same time – but unfortunately you're only allowed to peer through the windows. Opposite are the angular lines of the bright-white art gallery, the Edificio Estrella, which displays a rotating and representative sample of the prolific artist's work. Miró was nothing if not productive, and the Fundació holds 134 paintings, 300 engravings and 105 drawings, as well as sculptures, gouaches and preliminary sketches – more than six thousand works in all. There are no guarantees as to what will be on display, but you're likely to see a decent selection of his paintings, the familiar dream-like squiggles and half-recognizable shapes that are intended to conjure up the unconscious, with free play often given to erotic associations. The gallery also stores a comprehensive collection of Miró documents and occasionally hosts exhibitions.

Illetes and Platja Cala Comtesa

Well-heeled Illetes (sometimes written Illetas), just along the coast from Cala Major and 7km west of Palma, comprises a ribbon of restaurants, hotels and apartment buildings bestriding the steep hills that rise high above the rocky shoreline. There's precious little space left, but at least the generally low-rise buildings are of manageable proportions. A string of tiny cove beaches punctuates the coast, the most attractive being the pine-shaded Platja Cala Comtesa, at the southern end of the resort, alongside an out-of-bounds military zone.

Portals Nous

To the west of Illetes lies the larger resort of Portals Nous, a ritzy settlement where polished mansions fill out the green and hilly terrain abutting the coast. There's a tiny beach too, set beneath the cliffs and reached via a flight of steps at the foot of c/Passatge del Mar. The drawback is the main drag (also the MA-1C), which is disappointingly drab, but it does lead to the glitzy marina, one of Mallorca's most exclusive, where the boats look more like ocean liners than pleasure yachts – it's a favoured hang-out for the king and his cronies.

Palma Nova

Old Mallorca hands claim that Palma Nova, 4km west of Portals Nous, was once a

▼ PORTALS NOUS MARINA

beauty spot, and certainly its wide and shallow bay, with good beaches dotted amongst a string of bumpy headlands, still has its moments. But for the most part, the bay has been engulfed by a broad, congested sweep of hotels and tourist facilities. With the development comes a vigorous nightlife and a plethora of accommodation options on or near the seashore – though, as elsewhere, most are block-booked by tour operators throughout the season.

Magaluf

Torrenova, on the chunky headland at the far end of Palma Nova, is a cramped and untidy development that slides into Magaluf, whose high-rise towers march across the next bay down the coast. For years a bargain-basement package-holiday destination, Magaluf finally lost patience with its youthful British visitors in 1996. The local authorities won a court order allowing them to demolish twenty downmarket hotels in an attempt to end – or at least control – the annual binge of "violence, drunkenness and open-air sex" that, they argued, characterized the resort. The high-rise hotels were duly dynamited and an extensive clean-up programme subsequently freshened up the resort's appearance. However, short of demolishing the whole lot, there's not too much anyone can do with the deadening concrete of the modern town centre – and the demolished blocks will anyway be replaced, albeit by more upmarket hotels. These draconian measures have brought some improvement, but the resort's British visitors remain steadfastly determined to create, or at least patronize,

▲ BRITISH PUB, MAGALUF

a bizarre caricature of their homeland: it's all here, from beans-on-toast with Marmite to lukewarm pints of lager.

Aqualand and Western Water Park

May–Oct daily 10am–5/6pm; €19; ⓦ www.aqualand.es. Stuck on the western edge of Magaluf, Aqualand is a giant-sized water park with swimming pools, water chutes and flumes that rivals its sister Aqualand in S'Arenal (see p.76). Across the road is a second theme park, Western Water Park (May–Oct daily 10am–5/6pm; ⓦ www .western-park.com; €19.50). The main event here is a replica Wild West town – one of the most incongruous sights around – as well as a water park.

Cap de Cala Figuera

In contrast to most of the rest of the coast, the eastern reaches of the Cap de Cala Figuera, the pine-clad peninsula that extends south of Magaluf, have been barely touched by the developers, though the downside is that there is no

▲ PORTALS VELLS BEACH

public transport beyond the resort, so you have either to drive, walk or cycle. The clearly signposted road south onto the peninsula begins on the west side of Magaluf, where the *autopista* merges into the MA-IC. After about 1.5km, the road cuts past the Aqualand theme park (see p.79) and then keeps straight at a fork where the road to Santa Ponça (see opposite) curves off to the right. South of the fork, the road narrows into a country lane, passing a golf course before heading off into the woods. After about 4km, a steep, kilometre-long turning on the left leads down to Cala Mago (still signposted in Castilian as Playa El Mago), where a rocky little headland with a shattered guard house has lovely beaches to either side. Park and walk down to whichever cove takes your fancy: the nudist beach on the right with its smart café-restaurant, or the delightful pine-shaded strand on the left with its beach bar, tiny port and sprinkling of villas. Both provide sun loungers and showers.

Continuing a further 600m past the Cala Mago turning, you reach a second side road which cuts the 1km down to the cove beach of Portals Vells. Despite a bar-restaurant and a handful of villas, this remains a pleasant, pine-scented spot of glistening sand, rocky cliffs and clear blue water, especially appealing early in the morning before it gets crowded. Clearly visible from the beach are the caves of the headland on the south side of the cove.

A footpath leads to the most interesting, an old cave church where the holy-water stoup and altar have been cut out of the solid rock – the work of shipwrecked Genoese seamen, according to local legend.

Beyond the Portals Vells turning, the road continues south for 1.5km as far as a broken-down barbed-wire fence at the start of a disused military zone. You can't drive any further and you're not supposed to walk beyond the fence either, but some people do, braving the no-entry signs to scramble through the pine woods and out along the headland for about 1.5km to reach the solitary Cap de Cala Figuera lighthouse.

Santa Ponça

West of Magaluf, the MA-IC trims the outskirts of Santa Ponça, one of the less endearing of the resorts that punctuate this stretch of coast. Mostly a product of the 1980s, it's a sprawling conurbation where the concrete high-rises of yesteryear have been abandoned for a pseudo-vernacular architecture that's littered the hills with scores of suburbanite villas. That said, the setting is magnificent, with rolling green hills flanking a broad bay, whose spacious white sandy beaches offer safe bathing.

If you want to go diving, Zoea Mallorca, at the Club Náutico Santa Ponça, Via de la Cruz s/n (☎971 691444, ⓦwww.zoeamallorca.com) organizes dives and courses for all levels.

Peguera

Sprawling Peguera, about 6km from Santa Ponça, is strung out along a lengthy, partly pedestrianized main street – the Avinguda de Peguera – immediately behind several generous sandy beaches. There's nothing remarkable about the place, but it does have an easy-going air and is a favourite with families and older visitors. The MA-IC loops right round Peguera and the easiest approach, if you're just after the beach, is from the west: head into the resort along the main street and park anywhere you can before you reach the pedestrianized part of the Avinguda de Peguera, where the town's baffling one-way system sends you weaving through the resort's mazy side streets.

Cala Fornells

Two signed turnings on the west side of Peguera lead over to the neighbouring (and much prettier) resort of Cala Fornells. Take the more easterly turning and the road climbs up to a string of chic, *pueblo*-style houses that perch on the sea cliffs, which trail round to the tiny centre of the resort, where a wooded cove is set around a minuscule beach – and concreted sunbathing slabs. Cala Fornells does tend to get overcrowded during the daytime, but at night the peace and quiet return, which makes

▼ CALA FORNELLS

it a good base for a holiday, especially as it possesses a couple of particularly appealing hotels. You can also stroll out into the surrounding woods along a wide dirt track, which runs up behind the hotels, cutting across the pine-scented hills towards the stony cove beach of Caló d'es Monjo, 1km to the west.

Camp de Mar

Tucked away among the hills 3km west of Peguera, Camp de Mar has an expansive beach and fine bathing, though the scene is marred by the presence of two thumping great hotels dropped right on the seashore – the *Hotel Playa Camp de Mar*, a British favourite, and the smarter,

four-star *Hotel Riu Camp de Mar*, which caters mainly to Germans. Both are modern high-rises equipped with spacious, balconied bedrooms, and both can be booked only through packaging agents. The resort is also in the middle of a massive expansion, with brand-new villa complexes now trailing back from the beach in an all-too-familiar semi-suburban sprawl. All the same, the beach is an amiable spot to soak up the sun, and it's hard to resist the eccentric café stuck out in the bay and approached via a rickety walkway on stilts.

A minor road twists west from Camp de Mar over wooded hills to Port d'Andratx (see p.102).

▼ CAMP DE MAR

Accommodation

Hotel Bon Sol

Passeig d'Illetes 30, Illetes ☎ 971 402111, ⊛ www.ila-chateau.com /bonsol. Appealing, family-run hotel with pseudo-Moorish architectural flourishes that tumbles down the cliffs to the seashore – and its own artificial beach. It has all the conveniences you would expect from a four-star hotel, but the beach pool, surrounded by dense greenery, is especially appealing. The better rooms have fine views out over the bay. Its clientele is staid and steady, befitting the antique-crammed interior. About 8km from downtown Palma. Closed late Nov to late Dec. €170.

Hotel Cala Fornells

Platja Cala Fornells s/n, Cala Fornells ☎ 971 686950, ⊛ www.calafornells .com. Spick-and-span four-star hotel in a modern green-shuttered block overlooking the concrete sunbathing slabs of the resort's tiny beach. Ninety rooms, each neatly presented. Closed Nov & Dec. €150.

Hotel Coronado

Platja Cala Fornells s/n, Cala Fornells ☎ 971 686800, ⊛ www.hotelcoronado .com. Spruce, modern hotel block, where most of the 140 bedrooms have sea views and balconies. Smashing location above Cala Fornells' cove beach. Closed Nov & Dec. €150.

Hotel Nixe Palace

Avgda Joan Miró, Cala Major 269 ☎ 971 700888, ⊛ www.nixepalace .com. Once the haunt of the super-rich, the resort of Cala Major, about 5km west of downtown Palma, hit the skids until efforts were made to revamp the place in the 1990s. The prime example of the refit was the refurbishment of this hotel, a luxurious block with Art Deco references that backs onto the sea. Five-star hotel with all mod cons, including 24hr room service and swimming pools. €260.

Hotel Portixol

c/Sirena 27, Es Portixol ☎ 971 271800, ⊛ www.portixol.com. Es Portixol, just a couple of kilometres east of Palma cathedral, was once the preserve of the city's fishermen, who docked their boats at either of its sheltered coves – one is now a marina, the other is used by locals for sports and bathing. Es Portixol slipped into the doldrums in the 1960s, but it's now on the up, the trendsetter being this splendid Swedish-owned hotel, a very urban and urbane spot with all sorts of finessed details, from creative backlighting through to guest-room TV cabinets that look like mini-beach cabins. It's all good fun but note that it's worth paying extra for a room with a sea view. There's an outside swimming pool and an excellent restaurant, where you can dine either in or outside looking out at the sea. €210.

Restaurants

Flanigan's

Portals Nous harbour ☎ 971 679191 Lunch & dinner. One of the best – some would say *the* best – restaurant in Portals Nous. Nautical decor and international fusion cuisine with the emphasis on seafood. Seating is either in plush rooms inside or on the marina-facing terrace. Main courses from €20.

La Gran Tortuga

Aldea Cala Fornells 1, Peguera ☎971 686023. Lunch & dinner; closed Mon. This is the best restaurant in Peguera, overlooking the seashore on the (more easterly) road to Cala Fornells. It serves super seafood, has a terrace bar and even boasts its own swimming pool. A three-course evening meal will set you back about €35, but you can enjoy its excellent lunches for much less.

Méson Ca'n Torrat

c/Major 29, Calvià ☎971 670682. Dinner only from 8pm; closed Tues. Appealing little restaurant just down the hill from the church of Sant Joan Baptista. Specializes in roast leg of lamb and suckling pig. Moderate prices with main courses from around €17.

Tristán

Portals Nous harbour ☎971 675547. Lunch & dinner; closed Mon. Nouvelle cuisine is served up at this deluxe harbourside restaurant with two Michelin stars. Count on around €100 per person for dinner. Reservations essential.

Shopping

Fundació Pilar i Joan Miró

c/Joan de Saridakis 29, Cala Major. Mid-May to mid-Sept Tues–Sat 10am–7pm, Sun 10am–3pm; mid-Sept to mid-May Tues–Sat 10am–6pm, Sun 10am–3pm; ⊛miro.palmademallorca .es. Excellent museum shop selling everything from T-shirts, toys and ceramics to contemporary art books with the emphasis on the vast oeuvre of Joan Miró. For a description of the museum itself, see p.77.

Western Mallorca

Mallorca is at its scenic best in the gnarled ridge of the Serra de Tramuntana, the imposing mountain range which stretches the length of the northwest shore, with rearing peaks and plunging seacliffs intermittently punctuated by valleys of olive and citrus groves. Midway along is Sóller, an antiquated merchants' town that serves as a charming introduction to the region, especially when reached on the scenic train line from Palma. From Sóller, it's a short hop down to the coast to Port de Sóller, a popular resort on a deep and expansive bay, while the nearby mountain valleys shelter the bucolic stone-built villages of Fornalutx, Orient and Alaró, as well as the oasis-like gardens of the Jardins d'Alfàbia.

Alaró is also close to **Binissalem**, one of the most diverting little towns of the island's central plain, **Es Pla**. Southwest of Sóller, the principal coastal road, the MA-10, threads up through the mountains to reach the beguiling village of Deià and then Son Marroig, the mansion of the Habsburg archduke, Ludwig Salvator. Beyond lies the magnificent Carthusian monastery of **Valldemossa**, whose echoing cloisters briefly accommodated George Sand and Frédéric Chopin during the 1830s. From here, it's another short haul to the gracious *hacienda* of **La Granja**, and the picturesque mountain hamlets of **Banyalbufar** and **Estellencs**. Leaving the coast behind, you drift inland out of the mountains and into the foothills that precede the market town of **Andratx**, a crossroads town with easy

Trains, trams and buses

The 28-kilometre **train** journey from Palma to Sóller (☎971 752051, ⓦwww .trendesoller.com) is a delight, dipping and cutting through the mountains and fertile valleys of the Serra de Tramuntana. The line was completed in 1911 to transport oranges and lemons to Palma, at a time when it took a full day to make the trip by road. The rolling stock is tremendously atmospheric too, with narrow carriages – the gauge is only 914mm – that look like they've come out of an Agatha Christie novel. There are six departures daily from Palma station throughout the year and the ride takes just under an hour. A one-way ticket costs €9; €14 return. Trains from Palma link with the vintage trams that clunk down from Sóller to the coast at Port de Sóller, 5km away. Trams depart every half-hour or hour daily from 7am to 8pm and the fifteen-minute journey costs €3 each way.

There's a fast and frequent **bus** service from Palma to Sóller and Port de Sóller along the MA-11 road, which tunnels straight through the mountains as it approaches the coast. Another frequent bus links Palma with Sóller via Valldemossa, For bus timetable enquiries, call ☎971 177777, or check out ⓦtib.caib.es.

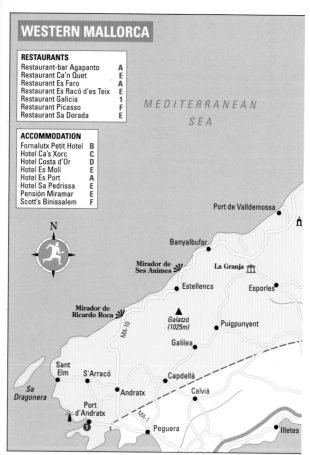

WESTERN MALLORCA

RESTAURANTS

Restaurant-bar Agapanto	A
Restaurant Ca'n Quet	E
Restaurant Es Faro	A
Restaurant Es Racó d'es Teix	1
Restaurant Galicia	F
Restaurant Picasso	E
Restaurant Sa Dorada	

ACCOMMODATION

Fornalutx Petit Hotel	B
Hotel Ca's Xorc	C
Hotel Costa d'Or	D
Hotel Es Molí	E
Hotel Es Port	A
Hotel Sa Pedrissa	E
Pensión Miramar	E
Scott's Binissalem	F

MEDITERRANEAN SEA

Port de Valldemossa

Banyalbufar

Mirador de Ses Animes

La Granja

Estellencs

Esporles

Mirador de Ricardo Roca

Galatzó (1025m)

Puigpunyent

Galilea

Sant Elm

S'Arracó

Capdellà

Calvià

Sa Dragonera

Andratx

Port d'Andratx

Peguera

Illetes

N

MA-10

MA-1

access to the tiny resort of **Sant Elm** and the larger harbour-cum-resort of **Port d'Andratx**. Most of the region's coastal villages have a tiny, shingle strip – nothing more. The twin **beaches** of Port de Sóller possess the longest strips of sand hereabouts, but the almost sand-less coves at Deià and Estellencs are much more appealing for their wild and wonderful setting.

Sóller

Sóller is one of the most laid-back and enjoyable towns on Mallorca, as well as being an ideal base for exploring the surrounding mountains. Rather than any specific sight, it's the general flavour of the place that appeals, with the town's narrow, sloping lanes cramped by eighteenth- and nineteenth-century fruit merchants' stone houses adorned with fancy grilles and big wooden doors.

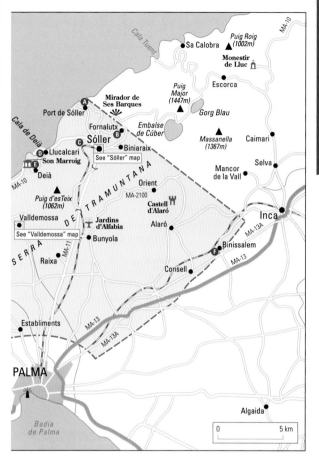

All streets lead to the main square, **Plaça Constitució**, an informal, pint-sized affair of crowded cafés and mopeds just down the hill from the train station. The square is dominated by the hulking mass of the church of **St Bartomeu** (Mon–Thurs 10.30am–1pm & 2.45–5.15pm, Fri & Sat 10.30am–1pm; free), a crude but somehow rather fetching Neo-Gothic remodelling of a medieval original – the most

appealing features are the enormous and precisely carved rose window high in the main facade and the apparently pointless balustrade above it. Inside, the cavernous nave is suitably dark and gloomy, the penitential home of a string of gaudy Baroque altarpieces.

Five-minutes' walk west is the **Museu Balear de Ciències Naturals** (Balearic Museum of Natural Sciences;

▲ MUSEU BALEAR DE CIÈNCIES NATURALS, SÓLLER

of modest displays. Temporary exhibitions occupy the top two floors and usually feature Balearic geology and fossils. The permanent collection is exhibited on the ground floor and is devoted to the leading botanists of yesteryear, including Archduke Ludwig Salvator (see p.96). The labelling is in Catalan, but English leaflets are available at the ticket desk, which also issues a free English-language brochure identifying and illustrating many species of local flora. This is a necessary introduction to the neat and trim Jardí Botànic (same hours), which rolls down the hillside in front of the house. The garden is divided into thirteen small areas, including Balearic species such as shade-loving plants in M4, mountain plants in M5 and dune and sea-cliff species in M2.

Tues–Sat 10am–6pm, Sun 10am–2pm; €5). Occupying an old merchant's house beside the main Palma–Sóller road, the interior has been stripped out to accommodate a series

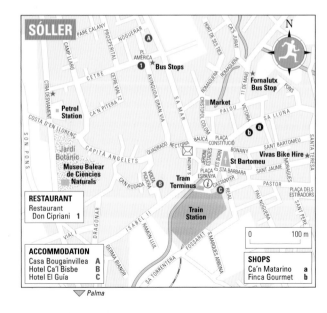

▽ Palma

Biniaraix and the Cornadors Circuit

Following c/Sa Lluna east from Sóller's main square, it takes about half an hour to stroll to the village of **Biniaraix**, passing orchards and farmland latticed with ancient irrigation channels and dry-stone walls. The village, nestled in the foothills of the Serra de Tramuntana, is tiny – just a cluster of handsome old stone houses surrounding a dilapidated church and the smallest of central squares – but it is extraordinarily pretty.

Biniaraix is also a useful starting point for **hiking** into the surrounding mountains, the most popular route being the stiff but scenic three-hour haul up the **Barranc de Biniaraix**, a beautiful ravine of terraced citrus groves; the trail starts 200m uphill from the square on c/Sant Josep. Sections of the *barranc* use the old **cobbled roadway** that was once part of the pilgrims' route between Sóller and the monastery at Lluc (see p.110).

Fornalutx

Fornalutx, a couple of kilometres east of Biniaraix along a narrow, signposted country lane, is often touted as the most attractive village on Mallorca, and it certainly has a superb location. Orange and lemon groves scent the valley as it tapers up towards the settlement, whose honey-coloured stone houses huddle against a mountainous backdrop. Matching its setting, the quaint centre of Fornalutx fans out from the minuscule main square, its narrow cobbled streets stepped to facilitate mule traffic, though nowadays you're more likely to be hit by a Mercedes than obstructed by a mule: foreigners love the place and own about half of the village's three hundred houses. This sizeable expatriate community sustains a clutch of cafés and restaurants and there are three enticing hotels, including the charming *Fornalutx Petit Hotel* (see p.103).

Port de Sóller

Port de Sóller is one of the most popular spots on the west coast, and its handsome, horseshoe-shaped bay, ringed by forested hills, must be one of the most photographed places on the island. The alcohol-fuelled high jinks of the Badia de Palma are a world away from this low-key, family-oriented resort, which is grafted onto an old fishing port and naval base. Attractions here include two pleasant strips of beach with generally clean and clear water, plus an excellent selection of restaurants. It's also worth making the enjoyable hour-long hike west to the lighthouse (*far*), which guards the cliffs of **Cap Gros** above the entrance to its inlet. From here, the views out over the wild and rocky coast and back across the harbour are truly magnificent, especially at sunset. There's a tarmac road all the way: from the tram terminus, walk round

▼ FORNALUTX

▲ PORT DE SÓLLER

the southern side of the bay past Platja d'en Repic and keep going, following the signs.

Trams from Sóller (see box on p.85) shadow the main road and clank to a stop beside the jetties, bang in the centre of Port de Sóller. From here, it's a couple of minutes' walk east to the tourist office, located beside the church at c/Canonge Oliver 10 (Mon–Fri 9am–1pm & 3–6.30pm, Sat 10am–1pm; ☎971 633042, Ⓦwww.sollernet .com), where you can pick up local information, including details of boat trips.

The Jardins d'Alfàbia

April–Sept Mon–Sat 9.30am–6.30pm; Oct–March Mon–Fri 9.30am–5pm & Sat 9.30am–1pm; €4.50. One of Mallorca's star turns, the **Jardins d'Alfàbia** are lush and beautiful terraced gardens set beside the southern entrance to the tunnel on the Palma–Sóller road. The gardens date back to the Spanish Reconquista, when a prominent Moor by the name of Benhabet was gifted the Alfàbia estate in return for supporting the Jaume I invasion. Benhabet planned his new estate in the Moorish manner, channelling water from the surrounding mountains to irrigate the fields and fashion oasis-like gardens. Generations of island gentry added to the estate without marring Benhabet's original design, thus creating the homogenous ensemble that survives today. From the roadside, you follow a stately avenue of plane trees towards the house. Before you reach it, you're directed up a flight of stone steps and into the gardens, where a footpath leads past ivy-covered stone

The Sa Firá i Es Firó

If you're around Port de Sóller in the second week of May, be sure to catch the **Sa Firá i Es Firó**, which commemorates the events of May 1561 when a large force of Arab pirates came to a sticky end after sacking Sóller. The Mallorcans had been taken by surprise, but they ambushed and massacred the Arabs as they returned to their ships and took grisly revenge by planting the raiders' heads on stakes. The story – bar decapitations – is played out in chaotic, alcoholic fashion every year at the festival. The re-enactment begins with the arrival of the pirates by boat, and continues with fancy-dress Christians and Arabs battling it out through the streets of the port, to the sound of blanks being fired in the air from antique rifles. The tourist office can give you a rough idea of the schedule of events, plus details of the dances and parties that follow.

walls, gurgling watercourses and brightly coloured flowers cascading over narrow terraces. Trellises of jasmine and wisteria create patterns of light and shade, while palm and fruit trees jostle upwards, allowing only the occasional glimpse of the surrounding citrus groves. At the end of the path, the gardens' highlight is a verdant jungle of palm trees, bamboo and bullrushes tangling a tiny pool. It's an enchanting spot, especially on a hot summer's day, and an outdoor bar sells big glasses of freshly squeezed orange juice.

A few paces away is the **house**, a rather mundane, verandahed *hacienda* whose handful of rooms house an eccentric mix of antiques and curios. Pride of place goes to a superb fourteenth-century oak chair adorned with delightful bas-relief scenes depicting the story of Tristan and Isolde. At the front of the house, the cobbled courtyard is shaded by a giant plane tree and surrounded by good-looking, rustic outbuildings. Beyond lies the gatehouse, an imposing structure sheltering a fine coffered ceiling of Mudéjar

▼ JARDINS D'ALFÀBIA

design, with an inscription praising Allah.

Bunyola and Orient

Just to the south of Alfàbia, a country road (the MA-2010 and then the MA-2100) forks east off the MA-11, looping past the plane trees and sun-bleached walls of the unassuming market town of **Bunyola** before snaking across the forested foothills of the Serra de Tramuntana. It's a beautiful (if occasionally nerve-jangling) drive and, after about 12km, you reach **Orient**, a remote hamlet of ancient houses scattered along the edge of the lovely Vall d'Orient. An especially beguiling spot, the village is framed by gentle hills covered with olive and almond groves.

The Castell d'Alaró

Beyond Orient, the MA-2100 sticks to the ridge overlooking the narrow valley of the Torrent d'en Paragon for around 3km, before veering south to slip between a pair of molar-like hills whose bare rocky flanks tower above the surrounding forest and scrub. The more westerly of the two sports the sparse ruins of the **Castell d'Alaró**, originally a Moorish stronghold but rebuilt by Jaume I. Visible for miles around, the castle looks impregnable on its lofty perch, and it certainly impeded the Aragonese invasion of 1285: when an Aragonese messenger suggested terms for surrender, the garrison's two commanders responded by calling the Aragonese king Alfonso III " fish-face", punning on his name in Catalan (*anfos* means "perch"). When the castle finally fell, Alfonso had the two roasted alive.

Access to the castle is from the south: coming from Orient, watch for the signposted right

▲ THE CASTELL D'ALARÓ

turn just beyond the Kilometre 18 stone marker. The first 3km of this side road are bumpy and narrow but reasonably easy, whereas the last 1.3km is gravel and dirt, with a perilously tight series of hairpins negotiating a very steep hillside – especially hazardous after rain. The road emerges at a car park and an old ramshackle farmstead, whose barn now holds the *Es Verger* restaurant. From the restaurant, the ruins of the castle are clearly visible it take about an hour and a half to walk up along a clearly marked track. The trail leads to the castle's stone gateway, beyond which lies an expansive wooded plateau accommodating the fragmentary ruins of the fortress, plus the tiny pilgrims' church of Mare de Déu del Refugi.

Alaró

On the MA-2100, it's about 1.5km south from the Castell d'Alaro turn-off to the town of **Alaró**, a sleepy little place of old stone houses fanning out from an attractive main square, Plaça Vila. A long and elegant arcaded gallery flanks one side of the square, and

a second is shadowed by the church, a fortress-like medieval affair whose honey-coloured sandstone is embellished with Baroque details.

Binissalem

Long the centre of the island's wine industry, **Binissalem** is an appealing country town on the northern peripheries of Mallorca's central plain, Es Pla. It's true that Binissalem looks dull and ugly from the old Palma–Alcúdia road, but persevere: the tatty, semi-industrial sprawl that straddles the main road camouflages an antique town centre, whose narrow streets contain a proud ensemble of old stone mansions dating from the seventeenth and eighteenth centuries. The old town zeroes in on its main square, Plaça Església, a pretty, stone-flagged piazza shaded by plane trees. The north side of the square is dominated by the Església Nostra Senyora de Robines, the clumpy, medieval nave of which is attached to a soaring Neo-Gothic bell tower added in 1908. Inside, the single-vaulted nave is dark and gloomy, its most distinctive features being its glitzy Baroque altarpiece and the grooved cockleshells, which are emblems of St James the Greater, one of the apostles.

Strolling southwest from the Plaça Església, along c/ Concepció, it's a few metres to the Ajuntament (Town Hall), and five minutes more to Can Sabater, c/Bonaire 25, one of the town's most distinguished patrician mansions. This was once the home of the writer Llorenç Villalonga (1897–1980), whose most successful novel was *The Dolls' Room*, an ambiguous portrait of Mallorca's nineteenth-century landed gentry in moral decline. In his honour, the house has been turned into the **Casa Museu Llorenç Villalonga** (Mon–Sat 10am–2pm, also Tues & Thurs 4–8pm; free), with detailed Catalan explanations of his life and times as well as his library and study. It also has its own chapel; the island's richer families usually had their own live-in priests.

Buses to Binissalem pull in beside the MA-13A, a few metres to the west of the foot of c/Bonaire, which leads straight to Plaça Església – a ten-minute walk in all, if that. Binissalem is also on the train line from Palma to Manacor with regular trains from both directions stopping at the station on the northern edge of the town centre. From the train station, it's a five- to ten-minute walk to the centre – proceed down c/S'Estació, turn right at the end and then left at the end of this second street to get to Plaça Església. Binissalem has no tourist office as such, but there are free town maps and brochures in the foyer of the Ajuntament – just help yourself. Binissalem also boasts one of Mallorca's finest hotels, *Scott's*, right in the centre of town at Plaça Església 12 – see p.105.

Deià

Deià, 10km west of Sóller, is beautiful. The mighty Puig d'es Teix (1062m) meets the coast here, and, although the mountain's lower slopes are now gentrified by the villas of the well-to-do, it retains a formidable, almost mysterious presence. Doubling as the coastal highway, Deià's main street, c/Arxiduc Lluís Salvador, skirts the base of the Teix, showing off most of the village's hotels and restaurants. Unfortunately, it's often too congested to be much fun, but the tiny heart of the village, tumbling over a high and narrow ridge on the seaward side of the road, still retains a surprising tranquillity. Here, labyrinthine alleys of old peasant houses curl up to a pretty country church, in the precincts of which is buried

▼ NOSTRA SENYORA DE ROBINES BINISSALEM

▲ DEIÀ

Robert Graves, the village's most famous resident. From the graveyard, there are memorable views out over the coast.

The Robert Graves house in Deià – Ca N'Alluny

Tues–Sun 10am–5pm; €5; timed visits by advance reservation on ☎971 636185, ⓦwww .fundaciorobertgraves.com. Robert Graves (see box opposite) put Deià on the international map, and his old home, **Ca N'Alluny**, a substantial stone building beside the main road about 500m east of the village, was opened to the public in 2006. For the most part, the house has been returned to its 1940s appearance and its rooms are decorated with Graves's own furnishings and fittings. A visit begins with a short film on the author's life and times and then come the period rooms. The study, where Graves produced much of his finest work, is of particular interest. Beyond is an exhibition room, with yet more biographical information and old photographs and manuscripts, and then it's on into the garden, where there are olive, carob, fruit and almond trees plus a small open-air theatre, where Graves and his chums were wont to read their poetry.

Deià Archeological Museum

Tues, Thurs & Sun 4–6pm; free; times may vary, confirm on ☎971 639001. Deià's other specific sight, its **Archeological Museum**, is hidden away in the wooded ravine below and between the old centre of the village and the *Hotel Es Molí* up on the main road. The archeologists William and Jacqueline Waldren founded the museum in 1962 to display the items they had retrieved from a number of local prehistoric sites. In particular, the couple had just hit the archeological headlines with their investigations into a prehistoric cave dwelling near Deià. Here they found a great hoard of bones, the remains of a veritable herd of *Myotragus balearicus*, a goat-like animal unique to the Balearics that seems to have been the nutritional mainstay here in prehistoric times. More importantly, the bones were found at a level in the subsoil that pushed back the date at which the earliest islanders were thought to have lived here by several hundred years – to 4000 or even 5000BC. The Waldrens have carried on with their archeological explorations ever since, and the museum displays many of the key finds from over forty years of work.

Cala Deià

Much loved by Graves, **Cala Deià**, is the nearest thing the village has to a beach, comprising some 200m of shingle at the back of a handsome rocky cove of jagged cliffs, boulders and white-crested surf. It's a great place for a swim, the water is clean, deep and cool, and there's a ramshackle beach bar (summer daily 12.30–5pm) to keep the swimmers happy. Most of the time, the cove is quiet and peaceful, but parties of day-trippers do sometimes stir things up. There are two ways to get there on foot. The more obvious route is signed from the bend in the road 80m or so northeast of the bus stop; it leads down a wooded ravine and takes about thirty minutes to complete - but remember to save some energy for the stiff walk back. Even more bucolic, however, is the path that threads its way through the wooded and terraced gulch in between the old centre of the village and the *Hotel Es Molí*; this takes about forty minutes. To drive there, head northeast along the main road out of Deià and watch for the sign about 700m beyond the *Hotel La Residencia*.

Son Marroig

Mon–Sat 9.30am–6pm; €3. South from Deià, the MA-10 snakes along the coast for 3km to reach **Son Marroig**, an imposing L-shaped mansion perched high above the seashore – and just below the road. The house dates from late medieval times, but it was refashioned in the nineteenth century to become the favourite residence of the Habsburg archduke Ludwig Salvator (1847–1915).

PLACES Western Mallorca

Robert Graves in Deià

The English poet, novelist and classical scholar **Robert Graves** (1895–1985) had two spells of living in Deià, the first in the 1930s, and the second from the end of World War II until his death. During his first stay he lived with Laura Riding, an American poet and dabbler in the mystical. Both married, the two had started their affair in England, where it created a furore, not as a matter of morality but because of its effects on the cabalistic and self-preoccupied literary-mystic group they had founded, the self-styled "Holy Circle". The last straw came when Riding, in her attempt to control the group, jumped out of a window, saying "Goodbye, chaps", and the besotted Graves leapt after her. The two both recovered, but the dottiness continued once they'd moved to Deià, with Graves acting as doting servant to Riding, whom he reinvented as a sort of all-knowing matriarch and muse. Simultaneously, Graves thumped away at his prose: he had already produced *Goodbye to All That* (1929), his bleak and painful memoirs of army service in the World War I trenches, but now came his other best-remembered books, *I, Claudius* (1934) and its sequel *Claudius the God* (1935), historical novels detailing the life and times of the Roman emperor.

At the onset of the Spanish Civil War, Graves and Riding left Mallorca to return to England, where Riding soon ditched Graves, who subsequently took up with a mutual friend, Beryl Hodge. Graves returned to Deià in 1946 and Hodge followed. They married in Palma in 1950, but did not live happily ever after. Graves had a predilection for young women, claiming he needed female muses for poetic inspiration, and although his wife outwardly accepted this waywardness, she did so without enthusiasm. Graves's international reputation ensured a steady stream of visitors to Deià from amongst the literati, but by the middle of the 1970s, Graves had begun to lose his mind, ending his days in sad senility.

Dynastically insignificant but extremely rich, the Austrian noble was a man in search of a hobby – and he found it in Mallorca. He first visited the island at the age of 19, fell head-over-heels in love with the place, and returned to buy this chunk of the west coast. Once in residence, Ludwig immersed himself in all things *Mallorquín*, learning the dialect and chronicling the island's topography, archeology, history and folklore in astounding detail. The Son Marroig estate comprises the house, its gardens and the headland below. The house boasts a handful of period rooms, whose antique furnishings and fittings are enlivened by a small sample of Hispano-Arabic pottery. On display too are some of the archduke's books and pen drawings, as well as several interesting photographs. The garden boasts gorgeous views along the jagged, forested coast and its terraces are graced by a Neoclassical belvedere of Tuscan Carrara marble.

▼ MONASTERY, VALLDEMOSSA

Down below the garden is a slender promontory, known as **Sa Foradada**, "the rock pierced by a hole", where the archduke used to park his yacht. The hole in question is a strange circular affair, sited high up in the rock face at the end of the promontory. It takes about forty minutes to walk the 3km down to the tip of land, a largely straightforward excursion to a delightfully secluded and scenic spot. Before you set out, you need to get permission at the house – as the sign on the gate at the beginning of the path (up the hill and to the left of the house) insists.

Valldemossa

The ancient hill-town of **Valldemossa** is best approached from the south. Here, with the mountains closing in, the road squeezes through a narrow, wooded defile before entering a lovely valley, whose tiered and terraced fields ascend to the town, a sloping jumble of rusticated houses and monastic buildings backed by the mountains. The origins of Valldemossa date to the early fourteenth century, when the asthmatic King Sancho built a royal palace here in the hills where the air was easier to breathe. Later, in 1399, the palace was gifted to Carthusian monks from Tarragona, who converted and extended the original buildings into a monastery, now Mallorca's most visited building after Palma cathedral. The monastery has always dominated Valldemossa, but the rest of the town is exceptionally pretty, a tangle of narrow cobbled lanes that tumble attractively down the hillside. It only takes a few minutes to explore them and

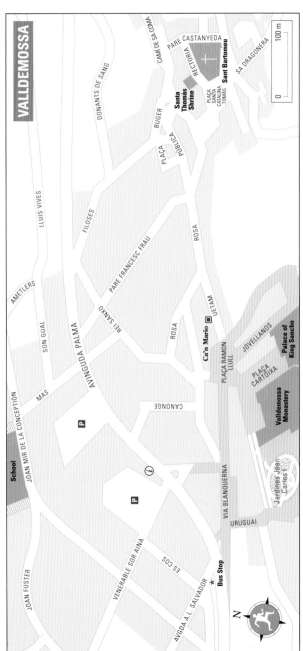

there are only two specific sights: the imposing Gothic bulk of the church of Sant Bartomeu and – round the back along a narrow alley at c/Rectoria 5 – the humble birthplace of Santa Catalina Thomàs, a sixteenth-century nun revered for her piety. The interior of the house has been turned into a simple little shrine, with a statue of the saint holding a small bird.

Valldemossa's Real Cartuja

March–May & Oct Mon–Sat 9.30am–5.30pm, Sun 10am–1pm; June & July Mon–Sat 9.30am–6.30pm, Sun 10am–1pm; Nov–Feb Mon–Sat 9.30am–4pm, Sun 10am–1pm; €7.50.

Today's **Real Cartuja de Jesús de Nazaret** (Royal Carthusian Monastery of Jesus of Nazareth) is mostly of seventeenth- and eighteenth-century construction, having been remodelled on several occasions. It owes its present notoriety almost entirely to the novelist and republican polemicist George Sand (1804–76), who, with her companion, the composer Frédéric Chopin, lived here for four months in 1838–39. They arrived just three years after the last monks had been evicted during the suppression of the monasteries, and so were able to rent a commodious set of vacant cells. Their stay is commemorated in Sand's *A Winter in Majorca*, a sharp-tongued and eagle-eyed epistle that is available hereabouts in just about every European language.

There's an obvious curiosity in looking around Sand's and Chopin's old quarters, but the monastery boasts far more interesting diversions, and it's easy to follow the multilingual signs around the place. A visit begins in the gloomy, aisle-less church, a square and heavy construction with a kitsch high altar and barrel vaulting that's distinguished by its late Baroque ceiling paintings. Beyond the church lie the shadowy cloisters, where the first port of call is the pharmacy crammed with beautifully decorated majolica jars, antique glass receptacles and painted wood boxes, each carefully inscribed with the name of a potion or drug. The nearby prior's cell is, despite its name, a comfortable suite of bright rooms, enhanced by access to a private garden with splendid views down the valley and graced by a wide assortment of religious *objets d'art*. Along the corridor, Cell no. 2 exhibits miscellaneous curios relating to Chopin and Sand, from portraits and a lock of hair to musical scores and letters. (It was in this cell that the composer wrote his "Raindrop" Prelude.) There's more of the same next door in Cell no. 4, plus Chopin's favourite piano which, after three months of unbelievable complications, only arrived just three weeks before the couple left for Paris. Considering the hype, these incidental mementoes are something of an anticlimax. Nor do things improve much in the ground-floor galleries of the adjacent Museu Municipal, which features local landscape painters. But don't give up: upstairs, the Museu Municipal Art Contemporani (same opening hours), holds a small but outstanding collection of modern art, including work by Miró, Picasso, Francis Bacon and Henry Moore, and a substantial sample of the work of the Spanish modernist Juli Ramis.

Back beside the prior's cell, be sure to take the doorway which leads outside the cloisters to the Palace of King Sancho. It's not the original medieval palace – that disappeared long ago – but this fortified mansion is the oldest part of the complex and its imposing walls, mostly dating from the sixteenth century, accommodate a string of handsome period rooms cluttered with faded paintings and other curios.

The palace has regular displays of folk dancing, and there are hourly free concerts of Chopin's piano music.

Port de Valldemossa

The closest spot to Valldemossa for a swim is **Port de Valldemossa**, a hamlet set in the shadow of the mountains at the mouth of a narrow, craggy cove. There's no public transport, but the drive down to the hamlet, once Valldemossa's gateway to the outside world, is stimulating: head west out of Valldemossa along the MA-10 and, after about 1.5km, turn right at the sign and follow the twisty side road for 6km down to the coast. Port de Valldemossa's beach is small and shingly, and tends to get battered by the surf, but the scenery is stunning.

La Granja

Daily: April–Oct 10am–7pm; Nov–March 10am–6pm; €9.50, €11.50 at peak periods. Nestling in a wooded and terraced valley some 10km from Valldemossa, the house and extensive grounds of **La Granja** are a popular tourist trip, but nonetheless the estate has managed to maintain a languorous air of old patrician comfort. La Granja was occupied until very recently by the Fortuny family, who took possession in the mid-fifteenth century, and,

after about the 1920s, it seems that modernization simply never crossed their minds. The main house holds a ramshackle sequence of apartments strewn with domestic clutter – everything from children's games and mannequins to old costumes, musical instruments and a cabinet of fans. There's also a delightful little theatre, where plays were once performed for the household in a manner common amongst Europe's nineteenth-century rural landowners. Likewise, the dining room, with its faded paintings and heavy drapes, has a real touch of country elegance, as does the graceful first-floor loggia. Look out also for the finely crafted, green-tinted Mallorcan chandeliers and the beautiful majolica tile-panels that embellish several walls.

▼ LA GRANJA

PLACES

Western Mallorca

Tagged onto the house, a series of workrooms recall the days when La Granja was profitable and self-sufficient. A wine press and almond and olive-oil mills prepared the estate's produce for export, whilst plumbers, carpenters, cobblers, weavers and sail-makers all kept pace with domestic requirements from their various workshops. The main kitchen is in one of the cellars, where you'll also find a grain store and a "torture chamber", an entirely inappropriate addition which holds a harrowing variety of instruments once regularly used by the Inquisition. Also of interest is the family chapel, a diminutive affair with kitsch silver-winged angels, and the expansive forecourt, which is surrounded by yet more antiquated workshops, where costumed artisans practise traditional crafts. This part of the visit is a bit bogus, but good fun all the same – and the home-made pastries and doughnuts (*bunyols*) are lip-smacking.

Esporles

Esporles, just a couple of kilometres from La Granja, is an amiable, leafy little town whose elongated main street follows the line of an ancient stone-lined watercourse. This is Mallorca away from the tourist zone, and although there's no special reason to stop, it's an attractive place to break any journey.

Puigpunyent and Galilea

Heading southwest from La Granja, a narrow and difficult country road heads up a V-shaped valley before snaking through the foothills of the Serra de Tramuntana mountains. After 10km you come to

Puigpunyent, a workaday farmers' village cheered up by a seventeenth-century church with a squat bell tower. Continuing southwest, the road threads along a benign valley of citrus groves and olive trees before wriggling its way on to **Galilea**, no more than an engaging scattering of whitewashed farmsteads built in sight of a stolid hilltop church.

From Galilea, it's another short but tortuous-verging-on-the-hair-raising drive to Andratx (see opposite).

Banyalbufar

The terraced fields of tiny **Banyalbufar** cling gingerly to the coastal cliffs beside the MA-10. The land here has been cultivated since Moorish times, with a spring above the village providing a water supply that's still channelled down the hillside along slender watercourses into open storage cisterns. The village is bisected by the MA-10, which doubles as the main street, flanked by whitewashed houses and narrow cobbled lanes. It culminates in the cute main square, perched above the MA-10 and overlooked by a chunky parish church dating from the fifteenth century. The village is a fine place to unwind and there's a rough and rocky beach fifteen minutes' walk away down the hill – ask locally for directions since the lanes that lead there are difficult to find.

Estellencs

About 1km southwest of Banyalbufar stands perhaps the most impressive of the lookout points that dot the coastal road, the **Torre del Verger**, a sixteenth-century watchtower built as a sentinel against pirate attack and now providing stunning views along the coast. **Estellencs**, 6km further on, is similar to Banyalbufar, with steep coastal cliffs and tight terraced fields, though if anything it's even prettier, its narrow, winding alleys adorned by old stone houses and a trim, largely eighteenth-century parish church – peep inside for a look at the exquisite pinewood reredos. A steep, but driveable, two-kilometre lane leads down from the village, past olive and orange orchards, to **Cala Estellencs**, a rocky, surf-buffeted cove that shelters a shingly beach and a summertime bar.

The Mirador de Ricardo Roca and Andratx

Heading southwest from Estellencs, the MA-10 threads along the littoral for 6km before slipping through a tunnel and – immediately beyond – passing the stone stairway up to the **Mirador de Ricardo Roca**. At 400m above the sea, this lookout point offers some fine coastal views, and you can wet your whistle at the restaurant next door. Beyond the *mirador*, the MA-10 makes a few final coastal flourishes before turning inland and worming its way up and over forested foothills to Andratx, a small and unassuming town where the main event is the Wednesday-morning market, a real tourist favourite. The old – and upper – part of **Andratx** is worth a few minutes, its medley of ancient stone houses and cobbled streets climbing up to the fortress-like walls of the parish church of Santa Maria, built high and strong to deter raiding pirates, its balustraded

precincts offering panoramic views down to the coast.

Sant Elm and Sa Dragonera

Parc Natural de Sa Dragonera. Daily: April–Sept 10am–5pm; Oct–March 10am–3pm; free. The low-key resort of **Sant Elm** is little more than one main street draped along the seashore, with a sandy beach at one end and a tiny harbour at the other. It's not an especially exciting place, but it's an amenable spot – with no high-rises – and there are frequent passenger ferries from its harbour to the austere offshore islet of **Sa Dragonera**, which is now protected as a *parc natural*.

From Sant Elm's minuscule harbour, **passenger boats** (Feb–April & Oct–Nov Mon–Sat 3 daily; May–Sept 4 daily; 15mins; €10 return; ☎639 617545 or ☎696 423933) take a few minutes to shuttle across

▼ ESTELLENCS

▲ SANT ELM

to the islet that comprises the **Parc Natural de Sa Dragonera**. For **sailing times**, call ahead or ask down at the harbour; Sant Elm tourist office has both schedules and island maps. This uninhabited hunk of rock, some 4km long and 700m wide, lies at an oblique angle to the coast, with an imposing ridge of seacliffs dominating its northwestern shore. Behind the ridge, a rough track travels the length of the island, linking a pair of craggy capes and their lighthouses. The boat docks at a tiny cove harbour about halfway up the east shore, which puts both ends of the island within comfortable walking distance, though the excursion north to **Cap de Tramuntana** is both shorter and prettier. There's also a much more challenging trail that clambers up to the **Na Pòpia** lighthouse on the northwest coast. Most people visit for the scenic solitude, but the island is also good for **birdlife** – ospreys, shags, gulls and other seabirds are plentiful, and you may also see several species of raptor. Incidentally,

be sure to make arrangements for your return boat trip on the outward journey.

Port d'Andratx

The well-appointed port and fishing harbour of **Port d'Andratx**, 6km southwest of Andratx, has been transformed by a rash of low-rise shopping complexes and Spanish-style villas. However, the heart of the old town, which slopes up from the south side of the bay, preserves a cramped network of ancient lanes, and there's no denying the prettiness of the setting, with the port standing at the head of a long and slender inlet flanked by wooded hills. Sunsets show the place to best advantage, casting long shadows up the bay, and it's then that the old town's gaggle of harbourside restaurants crowd with holidaymakers and expatriates. All in all, Port d'Andratx is an enjoyable place to spend a night or two, especially as it possesses several outstanding seafood restaurants and is easy to reach. The one thing it doesn't have, however, is a sandy beach – the nearest one is east over the hills at Camp de Mar (see p.82).

Accommodation

Casa Bougainvillea

c/Sa Mar 81, Sóller ☎971 633104, ⓦwww.casabougainvillea.com. This enjoyable B&B occupies a sympathetically modernized old, three-storey townhouse a short walk from Plaça Constitució. There are eight guest rooms here, all en suite, and each is decorated in a pleasingly unfussy style. Weather permitting, breakfast is served in the garden, where guests can idle away their time reading and relaxing. Very competitively priced too, with doubles and twins at €100.

Fornalutx Petit Hotel

c/Alba 22, Fornalutx ☎971 631997, ⓦwww.fornalutxpetithotel.com. This charming one-star hotel, with just eleven rooms, occupies an attractively furnished and spotlessly clean old stone house right in the centre of Fornalutx. The bonus is that the hotel's terraced garden has lovely views of the orchards behind.

▼ PORT D'ANDRATX

To get to c/Alba, walk down the main street from the village square and take the first left just beyond the conspicuous railings – a minute's stroll. €120.

Hotel Ca'l Bisbe

Bisbe Nadal 10, Sóller ☎971 631228, ⓦwww.hotelcalbisbe.com. This appealing four-star hotel occupies a sensitively updated former bishop's palace, complete with beamed ceilings, pool and garden. Each of the guest rooms is generously appointed with every mod con. €120.

Hotel Ca's Xorc

Ctra Sóller–Deià (MA-10) Km56.1 ☎971 638280, ⓦwww.casxorc .com. Located high in the hills, about 5km west of Sóller along the MA-10, this superb hotel occupies a renovated old olive mill in which each guest room has been decorated in sleek modern style. There's an outside pool and handsome terraced gardens, and the food is simply fabulous, featuring local ingredients and variations on traditional Mallorcan dishes. Reservations essential; closed mid-Nov to Feb. The smaller rooms start at €155, the most luxurious go for €280.

Hotel Costa d'Or

Llucalcari, near Deià ☎971 639025, ⓦwww.hoposa.es. This splendid four-star hotel occupies a wonderful setting, overlooking an undeveloped slice of coast and surrounded by pine groves and olive terraces just 2km east of Deia along the MA-10 coast road. There's a shaded terrace bar and a splendid outdoor swimming pool. The rooms are kitted out in slick, modern style and the best look out over the sea. Closed Nov–March. Doubles from €150.

Hotel El Guía

c/Castanyer 2, Sóller ☎971 630227, ⓦwww.sollernet.com/elguia. There may be several glossy new hotels in Sóller, but this long-established, two-star, family-run place is hard to beat. Set behind a pretty little courtyard, the hotel's layout and decor are very traditional and although the guest rooms are a tad spartan, they are perfectly adequate. To get there, walk down the steps from the train station platform and turn right. Closed Dec–Feb. €80.

Hotel Es Molí

Carretera Deià-Valldemossa s/n, Deià ☎971 639000, ⓦwww.esmoli .com. This long-established, four-star hotel has an excellent reputation, one that it fully deserves. The main building, which overlooks the main road from the wooded slopes at the very west end of Deià, is a postwar block whose lines are graced by arcaded galleries in the Spanish style. Inside, the public areas are smart, modern and roomy and are used to exhibit the work of local artists. All ninety well-appointed, air-conditioned bedrooms are tastefully decoarated; most have a balcony and many have wide coastal views. Amenities include gorgeous terraced gardens, an outside pool, a charming breakfast terrace and a minibus to take guests to the hotel's own (rocky) beach, a twenty-minute drive to the east. Closed Nov – March. Doubles from €200.

Hotel Es Port

c/Antoni Montis s/n, Port de Sóller ☎971 631650, ⓦwww.hotelesport .com. Arguably the best and certainly the most distinctive hotel in the port, this three-star establishment occupies a fortified country house that dates back to the seventeenth century. The interior displays many original features and the guest rooms are generally commodious and well appointed with traditional furnishings and fittings, though some are in the modern – and less appealing – annexe. The hotel sits in its own lush gardens at the back of the port, a few minutes' walk from the waterfront, and there's a large outside swimming pool. €100.

Hotel Sa Pedrissa

Carretera Deià-Valldemossa s/n, Deià ☎971 639111, ⓦwww.sapedrissa .com. This new hotel, about 2km west of Deià on the MA-10 coastal road, occupies an immaculately revamped old stone farmhouse, which, along with its assorted outhouses, perches high above – and has wide views over – the coast. Stone and marble floors, exposed wooden beams and oodles of white paint set the tone, there's a terrace pool and each of the nine bedrooms is impeccably turned out. Doubles from €120

Pensión Miramar

c/Ca'n Oliver s/n, Deià ☎971 639084, ⓦwww.pensionmiramar.com. You don't get many good deals in Deià, but this is one of them – a family-run *pension* in an old and traditional stone *finca* perched high above (and signposted from) the main road about halfway through the village. There are nine spartan if entirely adequate rooms here – some en suite and some with shared facilities – and the views over the village from the courtyard in front of the house are absolutely stunning. On foot, it takes about ten minutes to walk up from the main road. Closed Dec–Feb. Doubles from €70.

Scott's Binissalem

Plaça Església 12, Binissalem ☏971 870100, ⓦwww.scottshotel .com. One of Mallorca's finest hotels, *Scott's* sits right in the middle of Binissalem, a small town that has long been the centre of the island's wine industry. The hotel occupies an immaculately restored stone mansion that was originally owned by an almond grower, its sweeping stone arches and high ceilings enclosing three suites decorated in elegant, broadly nineteenth-century style. At the back, the old stone outbuildings surround a leafy courtyard and contain more recent rooms, each decorated in crisp modern style. Breakfast is served on a sunny terrace at the back of the hotel, and there's a swimming pool. Open all year. €175.

Restaurants

Restaurant-bar Agapanto

Camí Far 2, Port de Sóller ☏971 633860, ⓦwww.agapanto.com. Daily except Wed noon–4.30pm & 6.30pm–midnight. At the west end of Platja d'en Repic, beside the seashore at the start of the road up to the lighthouse, stands the *Agapanto,* a flashy, shaded very modish bar and restaurant dabbling in fusion food with ambient sounds to match. Vegetarian main courses, of which there is a good range, start at €13, a few euros more for the meat and fish. Also offers live music from salsa through to jazz.

Restaurant Ca'n Mario

c/Uetam 8, Valldemossa ☏971 612122. Closed Mon. In the *hostal* of the same name, this agreeable, family-run restaurant serves tasty traditional Mallorcan food at affordable prices – the (seasonal) asparagus with warm mayonnaise is a real treat. The *hostal* is situated in a delightful old stone house just a minute's walk from Valldemossa monastery – there's no sign for the restaurant, just go in through the *hostal* entrance and climb the stairs. Opening times are fairly elastic, which means you should make a reservation ahead of time.

Restaurant Ca'n Quet

Carretera Deià-Valldemossa s/n, Deià ☏971 639196. Tues–Sun 1–4pm & 8– 11pm. Closed Nov–March. Operated by, and situated just a couple of hundred metres west, of the *Hotel Es Molí* (see opposite), this smart restaurant serves up a creative menu featuring the very best of local ingredients, from fresh fish through to homegrown vegetables. The service is impeccable as are the views from the restaurant's wide, elevated terrace. Main courses €20 and up.

Restaurant Don Cipriani

Gran Via 43, Sóller ☏971 633049. Tues–Sun noon–3.30pm & 7.30–11pm. Arguably the best restaurant in town, this attractively decorated Italian place specializes in homemade pastas and pizzas, with main courses averaging around €16.

Restaurant Es Faro

Cap Gros, Port de Sóller ☏971 633752. Daily: March–Sept 11am–midnight, Oct–Feb 10am–5pm & 7–10pm, though out of season they sometimes close on one day a week. Set in a wonderful location, high up on the cliffs at the entrance to the harbour, this well-known restaurant offers spectacular views from its outside terrace. During the day, the *Es Faro* serves up coffees, light meals and an excellent *menú del día*, and at night it's à la carte with the seafood being much favoured. Mains from €20. An easy 1.7km drive – or stiff walk – up from Platja d'en Repic. Reservations strongly recommended in the evening.

Restaurant Es Racó d'es Teix

c/Vinya Vella 6, Deià ☎971 639501. Daily except Tues 1–3pm & 8–11pm.

Delightful Michelin-starred restaurant in an old stone house with an exquisite shaded terrace, located a steep 30m or so above the main road, about halfway into the village – watch for the sign. The Mediterranean fusion cuisine is memorable, as are the prices (up to €120 for a meal including wine, main courses from €30). Reservations well-nigh essential.

Restaurant Galicia

c/Isaac Peral 37, Port d'Andratx ☎971 672705. Daily noon–midnight. Highly recommended, bistro-style Galician place serving mouth-watering seafood

▼ RESTAURANT ES RACÓ D'ES TEIX

without the pretensions of some of its rivals down on the harbourfront. Especially strong on shellfish. Has simple, modern decor and very reasonable prices.

Restaurant Picasso

c/Pou Bo 20, Binissalem ☎971 870649. Mon–Sat 7–11.30pm. Outstanding, reasonably priced fusion cuisine is served here, in an old stone house with beamed ceilings about five minutes' walk from the town's main square, Plaça Església. The decor is idiosyncratic/ kitsch, the clientele buffed and polished. Main courses average around €20.

Restaurant Sa Dorada

c/Arxiduc Lluís Salvador 24, Deià ☎971 639509. Daily except Mon 1–4pm & 6.30–11.30pm. Opens at 7pm in winter. One of the best places in Deià for fish, with main courses from around €15. It's located about halfway into the village on the main road – you can eat either inside or on the terrace out at the back.

Shopping

Bodega José Luis Ferrer

c/Conquistador 103, Binissalem ☎971 511050, ⊛www.vinosferrer.com. Mon–Fri 9am–7pm, Sat 10am–2pm. José Luis Ferrer is the biggest wine producer on the island and the maker of the best island reds. If you book ahead, you can tour parts of the winery during the working week (Mon–Fri 2 daily; €6), but most visitors are content to visit the shop, which stocks the full range – and allows limited tastings (€0.90 per glass) – of the company's wines.

Ca'n Matarino

c/Sa Lluna 36, Sóller. Mon–Fri 10am–1pm & 4–7pm, Sat 10am–1pm. The best butchers in Sóller with all the usual offerings plus home-made *sobrasada* (sausages) and pâtés.

Finca Gourmet

c/Sa Lluna 16, Sóller. Mon–Fri 10am–1pm & 4–7pm, Sat 10am–1pm. Smashing delicatessen featuring all things Balearic from sausages and pastries to bread, olives and cheese.

PLACES

Western Mallorca

Northern Mallorca

The magnificent Serra de Tramuntana mountains reach a precipitous climax in the rearing peaks that bump along the coast of northern Mallorca. This is the wildest part of the island where even today the ruggedness of the terrain forces the main coastal road to duck and weave inland, offering only the most occasional glimpse of the sea. A rare exception is the extraordinary side road that snakes down to the attractive beach at Cala Tuent, as well as overcrowded Sa Calobra. But it's the well-appointed monastery of Lluc that remains the big draw here – for religious islanders and tourists alike.

Pushing on along the coast from Lluc, the MA-10 emerges from the mountains to reach Pollença, a tangle of stone houses clustered around a fine, cypress-lined pilgrims' way, the Way of the Cross. This appealing town is also within easy striking distance of both the comely coastal resort of Cala Sant Vicenç and the wild and rocky Península de Formentor, the bony, northernmost spur of the Serra de Tramuntana. The peninsula shelters the northern shore of the Badia de Pollença, where enjoyable Port de Pollença is a laid-back and family-oriented resort – in contrast to the more upbeat and flashy Port d'Alcúdia, hogging much of the next bay down, the Badia d'Alcúdia. In its turn, this port-resort is close to the old walled town of Alcúdia, which possesses a clutch of modest historical sights, and pocket-sized Muro, with its splendid main square and church. Back on the coast, the flow of the resorts is interrupted by the Parc Natural de S'Albufera, which takes the prize as the best birdwatching wetland in Mallorca. As regards beaches, there are long golden strands stretching round the bays of Pollença and Alcúdia and pretty cove beaches at Cala Sant Vicenç.

Gorg Blau

Heading northeast from Sóller, the MA-10 zigzags up into the mountains. After about 5km, it passes the steep turning down to Fornalutx (see p.89) before offering a last lingering look over the coast from the **Mirador de Ses Barques**. Thereafter, the road snakes inland and tunnels through the western flanks of Puig Major (1447m), the island's highest mountain. Beyond the tunnel is the **Gorg Blau** (Blue Gorge), a bare and bleak ravine that was a well-known beauty spot until a hydroelectric scheme filled it with puddle-like reservoirs. One of them is the Embalse de Cúber, an unappetizing expanse of water redeemed by its abundant birdlife, notably several different types of raptor. For a better look, follow the easy footpath which circumnavigates the reservoir; it takes a couple of hours to complete.

To the immediate north rear the craggy flanks of Puig Major, but the dramatic trail which twists up towards the summit from the military base beside the main road remains off-limits because of its radar station. This makes **Puig de Massanella** (1367m), which looms over the gorge to the east, the highest mountain that can be climbed on the whole of the island.

Cala Tuent

At the far end of the Gorg Blau the road tunnels into the mountains, to emerge just short of a left turn leading to **Cala Tuent** and Sa Calobra (see below). This turn-off makes for an exhilarating, ear-popping detour to the seashore, the well-surfaced road hairpinning its way down the mountain slopes so severely that at one point it actually turns 270 degrees to run under itself. About 10km down this road, there's a fork: head left over the hills for the 4km journey to the **Ermita de Sant Llorenç**, a tiny medieval church perched high above the coast, and Cala Tuent, where a smattering of villas clings to the northern slopes of Puig Major as it tumbles down to the seashore. Ancient orchards temper the harshness of the mountain, and the gravel and sand beach is one of the quietest on the north coast. It's a lovely spot to while away a few hours – if you can wrangle a parking spot (space is extremely limited) – and the swimming is safe provided you stay close to the shore.

Sa Calobra

Sa Calobra is a modern resort occupying a pint-sized cove in the shadow of the mountains. The setting itself is gorgeous, but the place is an over-visited disaster, and you'll have to pay €4 just to park. Almost every island operator deposits a busload of tourists here every day in summer and the crush is quite unbearable – as is the overpriced and overcooked food at the local cafés. The reason why so many people come here is to visit the impressive

▼ ROAD TO SA CALOBRA

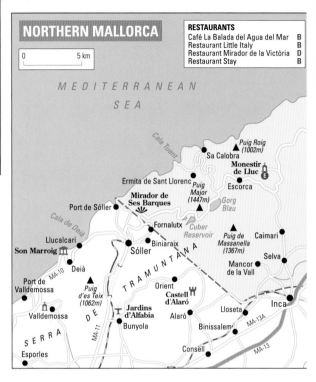

NORTHERN MALLORCA

0   5 km

RESTAURANTS	
Café La Balada del Agua del Mar	B
Restaurant Little Italy	B
Restaurant Mirador de la Victòria	D
Restaurant Stay	B

M E D I T E R R A N E A N
S E A

Cala Tuent

Puig Roig (1002m)
Sa Calobra
Monestir de Lluc
Escorca

Ermita de Sant Llorenç
Puig Major (1447m)
Gorg Blau
Mirador de Ses Barques
Port de Sóller
Cala de Deià
Fornalutx
Cuber Reservoir
Puig de Massanella (1367m)
Caimari
Biniaraix
Sóller
Llucalcari
Son Marroig
Selva
Deià
Mancor de la Vall
Port de Valldemossa
Puig d'es Teix (1062m)
Orient
Castell d'Alaró
Valldemossa
Jardins d'Alfabia
Alaró
Lloseta
Inca
Bunyola
Binissalem
T R A M U N T A N A
D E
S E R R A
Esporles
Consell
MA-10
MA-11
MA-13A
MA-13

box canyon at the mouth of the Torrent de Pareis (River of the Twins). It takes about ten minutes to follow the partly tunnelled walkway round the coast from the resort to the mouth of the canyon. Here, with sheer cliffs rising on every side, the milky-green river trickles down to the narrow bank of shingle that bars its final approach to the sea – though the scene is transformed after heavy rainfall, when the river crashes down into the canyon and out into the sea.

Monestir de Lluc

Daily: April–Sept 10am–11pm, Oct–March 10am–8pm; free. Tucked away in a remote valley about 35km northeast of Sóller, the austere, high-sided dormitories and orange-flecked roof tiles of the **Monestir de Nostra Senyora de Lluc** (Monastery of Our Lady of Lluc) stand out against the greens and greys of the surrounding mountains. It's a magnificent setting for what has been Mallorca's most important place of pilgrimage since the middle of the thirteenth century, when a local shepherd boy named Lluc stumbled across a tiny, brightly painted statue of the Virgin in the woods.

At the centre of the complex – pass through the monastery's double-doored entrance and keep straight on to the second

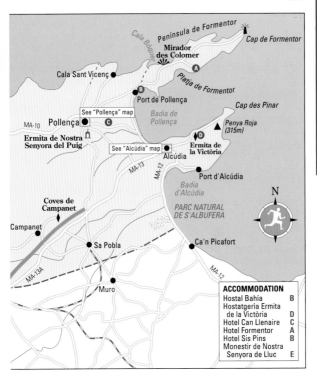

ACCOMMODATION

Hostal Bahía	**B**
Hostatgeria Ermita de la Victòria	**D**
Hotel Can Llenaire	**C**
Hotel Formentor	**A**
Hotel Sis Pins	**B**
Monestir de Nostra Senyora de Lluc	**E**

courtyard – is the main shrine and architectural highlight, the Basílica de la Mare de Déu de Lluc. Here, the basilica's elegant Baroque facade precedes a dark and gaudily decorated interior, dominated by heavy jasper columns. On either side of the nave, stone steps extend the aisles round the back of the Baroque high altar to a small chapel. This is the holy of holies, built to display the miraculously discovered statue of the Virgin, which has been commonly known as *La Moreneta* ("the Little Dark-Skinned One") ever since the original paintwork peeled off in the fifteenth century to reveal brown stone underneath. Just 61cm high, the Virgin looks innocuous, her face tweaked by a hint of a smile and haloed by a much

▼ MONESTIR DE LLUC

more modern jewel-encrusted gold crown. In her left arm she cradles a bumptious baby Jesus, who holds the "Book of Life", open to reveal the letters alpha and omega.

Every day, during the 11am Mass and again at evensong, the Escolania de Lluc, a boys' choir founded in the early sixteenth century with the stipulation that it must be "composed of natives of Mallorca, of pure blood, sound in grammar and song", performs in the basilica. They're nicknamed *Els Blauets*, "The Blues", for the colour of their cassocks.

Museu de Lluc

Daily: 10am–1.30pm & 2.30–5pm; €3. Just inside and to the right of the basilica's main entrance a small door leads through to a corridor that runs past the stairway up to the enjoyable **Museu de Lluc** (Lluc Museum). After the ticket desk, this begins with a modest section devoted to archeological finds from the Talayotic and Roman periods, and then it's on into the so-called Sala del Tresor (Treasure Room), packed with all manner of folkloric items brought here

to honour *La Moreneta*, from fancily painted fans, medallions, rosaries and crosses through to walking sticks discarded when the supplicants found they were no longer lame. Beyond, a room of incidental bric-a-brac, featuring examples of traditional island costume, precedes a substantial collection of *majolica* (see box below), glazed earthenware mostly shaped into two-handled drug jars and show dishes or plates. Some two or three hundred pieces are on display, the pick coming from the eighteenth century, when the decoration varied in sophistication, from broad and bold dashes of colour to carefully painted naturalistic designs, but the colours remained fairly constant, restricted by the available technology to iron red, copper green, cobalt blue, manganese purple and antimony yellow. There is also a good sample of Balearic and Valencian lustreware, brown earthenware with a sheen – or lustre – and manufactured between the sixteenth and the eighteenth centuries. The final rooms on this floor are, by comparison, rather disappointing, devoted

Majolica

The fifteenth century witnessed a vigorous trade in decorative pottery sent from Spain to Italy via Mallorca. The Italians coined the term "*majolica*" to describe this imported Spanish pottery after the medieval name for the island through which it was traded, but thereafter the name came to be applied to all tin-glazed pottery. The process of making *majolica* began with the mixing and cleaning of clay, after which it was fired and retrieved at the "biscuit" (earthenware) stage. The biscuit was then cooled and dipped in a liquid glaze containing tin and water. The water in the glaze was absorbed, leaving a dry surface ready for decoration. After painting, the pottery was returned to the kiln for a final firing, which fused the glaze and fixed the painting. Additional glazings and firings added extra lustre. Initially, *majolica* was dominated by greens and purples, but technological advances added blue, yellow and ochre in the fifteenth century. *Majolica* of one sort or another was produced in Mallorca up until the early twentieth century.

to the uninspiring island land- and village-scapes of José Coll Bardolet (1912–92).

Upstairs – and this is a bit of a surprise – the museum displays an excellent sample of Mallorcan art, either by native artists or artists once resident here. Amongst them, there are the Goya-esque works of Salvador Mayol (1775–1834); the Neo-Impressionist canvases of Llorenç Cerdà (1862–1955); the romantic landscapes of Bartomeu Sureda (1769–1851); and the finely observed mountain landscapes of Antoni Ribas (1845–1911), arguably the most talented artist on display here.

Lluc's Camí dels Misteris del Rosari

From outside the monastery's double-doored entrance, walk a few metres to the west and you'll soon spot the large, rough-hewn column at the start of the **Camí dels Misteris del Rosari** (Way of the Mysteries of the Rosary), a broad pilgrims' footpath that winds its way up the rocky hillside directly behind the monastery. Dating from 1913, the solemn granite stations marking the route are of two types: simple stone pyramids and, more intriguingly, rough trilobate columns of Gaudí-like design, each surmounted by a chunky crown and cross. The prettiest part of the walk is round the back of the hill where the path slips through the cool, green woods with rock overhangs on one side and views out over the bowl-shaped Albarca valley on the other. It takes about ten minutes to reach the top of the hill, where a wrought-iron *Modernista* cross stands protected by ugly barbed wire. Afterwards it's possible to

stroll down into the Albarca valley by following the country road that begins to the left of the monastery's main entrance. The valley is shadowed by Puig Roig (1002m), but there's nowhere in particular to aim for and the road fizzles out long before you reach the coast.

Lluc's Jardí Botànic

Mon–Sat 10am–1pm & 3–6pm; free. On the east side of the monastery are the **Jardí Botànic** (Botanical Gardens) – they're signed through the conspicuous arches on the right as you face the main building. The gardens are laid out with local plants as well as exotics, plus small ponds and waterfalls, little footbridges and even a windmill. It takes about fifteen minutes to walk through the gardens on a well-defined path.

Pollença

The lovely little town of **Pollença** nestles among a trio of humpy hillocks where the coastal mountains fade into flatland some 20km from Lluc. Following standard Mallorcan practice, the town was established a few kilometres from the seashore to guard against sudden pirate attack, with its harbour, Port de Pollença (see p.117), left unprotected. For once the stratagem worked. Pollença successfully repelled a string of piratical onslaughts and the dignified stone houses that cramp the twisting lanes of the centre today date back to the seventeenth and eighteenth centuries.

In the middle, **Plaça Major**, the amiable main square, accommodates a cluster of laid-back cafés and is the site of a lively Sunday-morning fruit

▲ POLLENÇA MARKET

and veg market. Overlooking the square is the severe façade of the church of **Nostra Senyora dels Àngels**, a sheer cliff-face of sun-bleached stone pierced by a rose window. Close by, behind the church on the north side of the centre, is Pollença's pride and joy, its **Via Crucis** (Way of the Cross), a long, steep and beautiful stone stairway, graced by ancient cypress trees which ascends the Puig de Calvari (Calvary Hill). At the top, a much-revered statue of Mare de Déu del Peu de la Creu (Mother of God at the Foot of the Cross) is lodged in a simple, courtyarded *oratori* (chapel), from

▼ VIA CRUCIS, POLLENÇA

where the views out over the coast and town are sumptuous. On Good Friday, a figure of Jesus is slowly carried by torchlight down from the *oratori* to the aforementioned church of Nostra Senyora, a solemn and moving procession known as the *Davallament* (Lowering).

Take c/Antoni Maura from Plaça Major and you soon reach a leafy square, whose greenery surrounds an antique water wheel and a stumpy, much battered watchtower. Behind looms the austere façade of **Nostra Senyora del Roser**, a deconsecrated church with a bright and gaudy Baroque interior that is sometimes used for temporary exhibitions. Otherwise, the church is usually closed, but the adjoining cloisters form part of the **Museu de Pollença** (Tues–Fri 10.30am–1pm, Sat & Sun 11am–1pm, but hours extended during exhibitions; free), which houses a surprisingly good and regularly rotated collection of contemporary paintings, photography and video art, including pieces by winners of the town's annual art competition. There's also a modest assortment of local archeological finds, though these are poorly labelled, and a

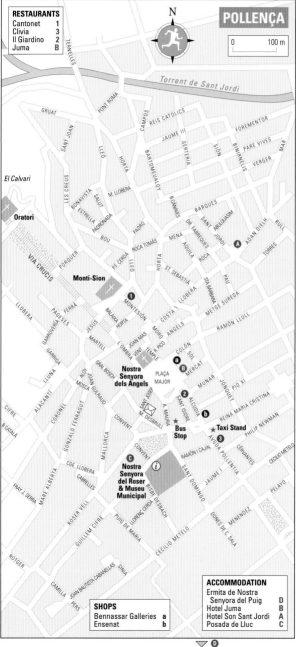

RESTAURANTS
Cantonet	1
Clivia	3
Il Giardino	2
Juma	B

POLLENÇA

0   100 m

N

Torrent de Sant Jordi

El Calvari

Oratori

Monti-Sion

VIA CRUCIS

Nostra Senyora dels Àngels

PLAÇA MAJOR

Bus Stop

★ **Taxi Stand**

Nostra Senyora del Roser & Museu Municipal

SHOPS
Bennassar Galleries	a
Ensenat	b

ACCOMMODATION
Ermita de Nostra Senyora del Puig	D
Hotel Juma	B
Hotel Son Sant Jordi	A
Posada de Lluc	C

116

room of Mallorcan Primitives, paintings, most memorably a warm, tender and exquisitely detailed *Virgin and Musical Angels* by Francesc Comes (1379–1415). In the cloisters, look out for the memorial to Philip Newman (1904–66), the Manchester-born violinist who took a real shine to Pollença in the 1950s, founding and fostering its main musical festival, the Festival de Pollença, still held here every year throughout July and August (℡971 535077, ⓦwww .festivalpollenca.org).

Ermita de Nostra Senyora del Puig

There are magnificent views from the **Ermita de Nostra Senyora del Puig** (Hermitage of Our Lady of the Hill), a rambling, mostly eighteenth-century monastery perched on top of the Puig de Maria, a 320-metre-high hump facing the south end of Pollença. The monastic complex, with its fortified walls, courtyard, chapel, refectory and cells, has had a chequered history, alternately abandoned and restored by both monks and nuns. The Benedictines now own the place, but the monks are gone and today a custodian supplements the order's income by renting out cells to tourists (see p.124). There's nothing specific to see, but the setting is extraordinarily serene and beautiful, with the mellow honey-coloured walls of the monastery surrounded by ancient carob and olive trees, a

million miles from the tourist resorts visible far below.

It takes around an hour to walk to the monastery from the centre of town. Take the signposted turning off the main Pollença–Inca road just south of town and head up this steep lane until it fizzles out after 1.5km, to be replaced by a cobbled footpath which winds up to the monastery's entrance. It's possible to drive to the top of the lane, but unless you've got nerves of steel, you're better off parking elsewhere. Note that there have been reports of cars left overnight at the foot of the lane being vandalized; although this is unusual, you might prefer to park in town instead.

Cala Sant Vicenç

Love or hate the place – and opinions are equally divided – there's no denying that **Cala Sant Vicenç**, a modern

▼ CALA SANT VICENÇ

▲ PORT DE POLLENÇA BEACH

6km-long hike takes around three hours; the first part uses a rough stone road, the second follows a well-defined path that leads to the base of Puig de l'Àguila – but you'll still need a proper hiking map to find your way.

Port de Pollença

With the mountains as a shimmering backcloth, **Port de Pollença** is a pleasantly low-key, family-oriented resort that arches through the flatlands behind the Badia de Pollença. The beach is the focus of attention here, a narrow, elongated sliver of sand, which is easily long enough to accommodate the crowds, while its sheltered waters are ideal for swimming. A rash of apartment buildings and hotels blights the edge of town, and the noisy main road to Alcúdia cuts through the centre, but there are no high-rises to speak of and the resort is dotted with attractive whitewashed and stone-trimmed villas. All together it's quite delightful, especially to the north of the marina, where a portion of the old beachside road – along Passeig Anglada Camarasa and Passeig Voramar – has been pedestrianized. If you get bored of the beach, you can also hire a bike and cycle out into the surrounding countryside or make the enjoyable hike across the neck of the Formentor peninsula to Cala Bóquer, or catch one of the summertime, shuttle passenger ferries from the marina to the Platja de Formentor (€9 return; see p.118).

resort 6km northeast of Pollença, boasts an attractive, solitary setting amongst bare rocky outcrops that nudge gingerly out into the ocean. The problem is the resort itself: some visitors like the modern villas that spill over and around the wooded ravine at its heart, others think they are dreary in the extreme, but no one likes the *Hotel Don Pedro*, crassly plonked on the minuscule headland separating the resort's two small but sandy beaches. But, the resort is still a pleasant spot for a swim – the water is crystal clear and the beach is sheltered from the wind. In addition, you can hike out onto the wild and wind-licked seashore. The obvious targets are the remote *calas* that punctuate the coastline, but you could also undertake the moderately strenuous hoof up to the top of Puig de l'Àguila (206m), from where there are grand views over the surrounding shoreline. This

The Península de Formentor

Heading northeast out of Port de Pollença, Carretera Formentor clears the military zone at the far end of the resort before weaving up into the hills at the start of the twenty-kilometre-long **Península de Formentor**, the final spur of the Serra de Tramuntana. At first, the road – which suffers a surfeit of tourists from mid-morning to mid-afternoon – offers extravagant views back over the Badia de Pollença, but this is merely a foretaste of what lies beyond. The first place to stop, about 4km from town, is the **Mirador de Mal Pas**, where a string of lookout points perch on the edge of plunging, north-facing seacliffs.

Beyond the *mirador*, the road cuts a handsome route as it threads its way along the coast, somehow negotiating the sheerest of cliffs before slipping down to a fork in the road, where it's straight on for the cape (see below) and right for the *Hotel Formentor* (see p.124). The fork also marks the start of the **Platja de Formentor**, a narrow strip of golden sand

that stretches east for about 1km beneath a low, pine-clad ridge. It's a beautiful spot, with views over to the mountains on the far side of the bay, though it can get a tad crowded in the height of the season. Most visitors drive here, using the large car park beside the fork in the road, but it's possible to arrive by boat from Port de Pollença (see p.117), or bus from Alcúdia and Port de Pollença (May–Oct Mon–Sat 4 daily); buses stop beside the car park, the briefest of walks from the beach.

Beyond the fork, the main peninsula road runs through woods before clambering upwards, tunnelling through Mont Fumat to emerge on the rocky mass of the **Cap de Formentor**, a tapered promontory of bleak seacliffs and scrub-covered hills. From the silver-domed lighthouse stuck on the cape's windswept tip, there are magnificent views and good birdwatching. Ravens, martins and swifts often circle overhead and during the spring and summer migrations, thousands of seabirds fly over the cape, Manx and Cory's

▼ PENÍNSULA DE FORMENTOR

shearwaters in particular. If you fancy a snack before heading back from the cape, there's a (very average) café in part of the lighthouse.

Alcúdia

To pull in the day-trippers, pint-sized **Alcúdia** wears its history on its sleeve. The crenellated wall that encircles much of the town centre is a modern restoration of the original medieval defences, and although the sixteenth- to eighteenth-century townhouses behind it are genuine enough, the whole place is inordinately spick and span. Situated on a neck of land separating two large and sheltered bays, the site's strategic value was first recognized by the Phoenicians, who settled here in around 700 BC, but they were displaced by the Romans, who built their island capital, Pollentia, on top of the earlier settlement. The Moors built a fortress here in about 800AD, naming it Al Kudia (On the Hill), and thereafter the town prospered as a trading centre, a role it performed well into the nineteenth century, when it

▲ ALCÚDIA TOWN WALLS

slipped into a slow decline – until tourism refloated the local economy.

It only takes an hour or so to explore Alcúdia's compact centre, beginning at the old town's eastern entrance, on Plaça Carles V, from where you'll soon reach the tiny main square, Plaça Constitució and its pavement cafés. Just beyond, on c/Major, is Alcúdia's best-looking building, the **Ajuntament** (Town Hall), a handsome, largely seventeenth-century structure with an

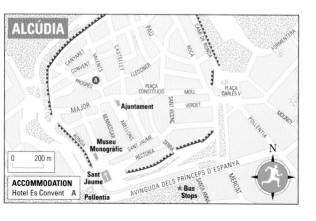

elegant stone balcony and overhanging eaves.

From c/Major, it's a brief walk to the southwest corner of the old town and the fascinating **Museu Monogràfic**, c/Sant Jaume 2 (July–Oct Tues–Fri 10am–3pm, Sat & Sun 10.30am–1pm; Nov–June Tues–Fri 10am–4pm, Sat & Sun 10.30am–1pm; €2, which includes admission to Pollentia – see below). The museum consists of just one large room, but it's stuffed with a satisfying assortment of archeological bits and bobs, primarily Roman artefacts from Pollentia, including amulets, miniature devotional objects, tiny oil lamps and, remarkably enough, a gladiator's helmet. Across the street, dominating this portion of the old town, is the heavyweight and heavily reworked Gothic church of **Sant Jaume**, which holds a modest religious museum (May–Oct Tues–Fri 10am–1pm; €1).

Alcúdia's Roman ruins

Across the ring road from the church of Sant Jaume lie the broken pillars and mashed-up walls of Roman **Pollentia** (same times and ticket as the Museu Monogràfic). The Vandals ransacked the Roman city in 426 and thereafter the locals helped themselves to the rest of the stone, so it takes a lot of imagination to discern the layout of the former capital, though the signs do their best. By contrast, the open-air remains of the **Teatre Romà** (Roman Theatre; open access; free) are much more substantial. Dating from the first century BC, this is the smallest of the twenty Roman theatres to have survived in Spain. Nonetheless, despite its modest proportions, the builders were able to stick to the standard type of layout with eight tiers of seats carved out of the rocky hillside, divided by two gangways. Inevitably, the stage area, which was constructed of earth and timber, has disappeared, but getting the flavour of the place is easy enough. It's a pleasant spot too, the ruins set amidst fruit and olive trees, a ten-minute stroll to the south of the old town. The short, signed footpath to the Roman theatre leads along c/Santa Anna, a pretty country lane lined by old stone walls that runs south from the ring road a couple of hundred metres east of the remains of Pollentia.

The Ermita de la Victòria

East of Alcúdia a steep and rocky promontory pokes a wild finger out into the sea, the first part of its northern shore traversed by a narrow road, which begins at the easternmost intersection on Alcúdia's ring road. This promontory road slips past the marina and suburban villas of **Bonaire** before emerging into more scenic terrain, offering fine views of the Badia de Pollença as it bumps over the steep, pine-clad ridges that fringe the coast. After about 5km, a signed turning on the right climbs 700m up the wooded hillside to the **Ermita de la Victòria**, a fortress-like church with a simple, single-vault nave, built in the seventeenth century to hold and protect a crude, but much-venerated, statue of the Virgin. It was a necessary precaution: this part of the coast was especially prone to attack and, even with these defences, pirates still stole the statue twice, though on both occasions the islanders eventually got it back. Part of the Ermita has been turned into an excellent and inexpensive hotel (see p.124) and there's a first-rate restaurant here too (see p.126). Furthermore, the *santuari* is the starting point for **hikes** further along the promontory, whose severe peaks are dotted with ruined defensive installations. The obvious draw is the 315-metre **Sa Penya Roja** mountain, from whose summit there are more great views. The outward part of the hike, leading up through woods and beneath steep cliffs, is quite strenuous; return is by the same route; allow thirty to 45 minutes each way. It begins on the wide dirt road that climbs up behind the *santuari*, but the later sections are on trails that require a hiking map.

Port d'Alcúdia

Port d'Alcúdia, 2km south of Alcúdia, is easily the biggest and busiest of the resorts in the north of the island, a seemingly interminable string of high-rise hotels and apartment buildings served by myriad restaurants and café-bars. Despite the superficial resemblance, however, Port d'Alcúdia is a world away from the seamy resorts of the Badia de Palma: the tower blocks are relatively well distributed, the streets are neat and tidy, and there's a prosperous and easy-going air, with families particularly well catered for. Predictably, the daytime focus is the beach, a superb arc of pine-studded golden sand which stretches south round the Badia d'Alcúdia from the two purpose-built jetties of Port d'Alcúdia's combined marina, cruise-boat and fishing harbour. A tourist "train" (on wheels) runs up and down the length of the resort every hour from June to September, transporting sunbaked bodies from one part of the beach to another. There's very little to distinguish anywhere from anywhere else but the numbered palm-thatched *balnearios* (beach bars) are a great help in actually remembering where you are. A walkway runs along the back of the beach, which is usually more crowded to the north.

Just as crowded, and located a kilometre or so inland along Avinguda del Tucan, is the much-vaunted **Hidropark**, a gigantic pool complex with all sorts of flumes and chutes (May–Oct daily 10.30am–6pm; ☎971 891672, ⓦwww .hidropark.com; €15 for 12 year olds plus, €8 for 5–11 year olds).

There's a superabundance of car, moped and bike rental

▼ PORT D'ALCÚDIA BEACH

companies strung out along the main drag, the Carretera d'Artà, and summer boat trips, leaving from the marina, make frequent explorations of the rocky, mountainous coastline to the northeast.

The Parc Natural de S'Albufera

Daily: April–Sept 9am–6pm; Oct–March 9am–5pm; free. Given all the high-rise development along the Badia d'Alcúdia, the pristine wetland of the two-thousand-acre **Parc Natural de S'Albufera** makes a wonderful change. Swampland once extended round much of the bay, but large-scale reclamation began in the nineteenth century, when a British company dug a network of channels and installed a steam engine to pump the water out. These

▼ PARC NATURAL DE S'ALBUFERA

endeavours were prompted by a desire to eradicate malaria – then the scourge of the local population – as much as by the need for more farmland. Further drainage schemes accompanied the frantic tourist boom of the 1960s, and only recently has the Balearic government organized a park to protect what little remains.

The park entrance is clearly signposted on the MA-12, about 6km southeast along the coast from Port d'Alcúdia's marina. From the entrance, a country lane leads just over 1km inland to the reception centre, Sa Roca, where you can pick up a free map and introductory leaflet. There's a small wildlife display in the adjacent building. Note that you can't drive down the country lane; the best bet is to cycle here or take a bus to the entrance and walk – lots of buses from Port d'Alcúdia stop near the entrance. If you do bring a vehicle, you'll find a small roadside parking area just east of the entrance.

Footpaths and cycle trails head out from Sa Roca into the reedy, watery tract beyond, where a string of well-appointed hides allow excellent birdwatching. Over two hundred different types of birds have been spotted, including resident wetland-loving birds from the crake, warbler and tern families; autumn and/or springtime migrants such as grebes, herons, cranes, plovers and godwits; and wintering egrets and sandpipers. Such rich pickings attract birds of prey in their scores, especially kestrels and harriers.

Muro

From the MA-12 on the west side of Ca'n Picafort, an easy country road heads west across a pancake-flat, windmill-studded hinterland to reach the hilltop town of **Muro**, a sleepy little place dotted with big old townhouses built by wealthy landowners. The best time to be here is on the **Revetla de Sant Antoni Abat** (Eve of St Antony Abbot's Day), January 16, when locals gather round bonfires to drink and dance, tucking into specialities like sausages and eel pies (*espinagades*).

At other times of the year, allow an hour or two to explore the town, beginning with its handsome main square, **Plaça Constitució**, an attractive open area flanked by old stone houses. The square is also overseen by the ponderous hulk of the church of **St Joan Baptista**, a real hotchpotch of architectural styles, its monumental Gothic lines uneasily modified by the sweeping sixteenth-century arcades above the aisles. A slender arch connects the church to the adjacent belfry, an imposing seven-storey construction partly designed as a watchtower. The church's cavernous interior holds a mighty vaulted roof and an immense altarpiece, a flashy extravaganza of columns, parapets and tiers in a folksy rendition of the Baroque.

From the main square, it's a couple of minutes' walk east to the **Museu Etnològic**, c/ Major 15 (Tues–Sat 10am–3pm & Sun 10am–2pm; €3), set in a rambling old mansion and displaying a motley assortment of local bygones, such as old agricultural implements and traditional costumes. Among the pottery, look out for the *siurells*, miniature white-, green- and red-painted figurines created in a naive style. Once given as presents, but now debased as a mass-produced tourist trinket, these are whistles – hence the spout with the hole – shaped in the form of animals, humans and mythological or imaginary figures. That's just about it for Muro, though on a hot summer's day you'll be glad of a drink at one of the cafés around the main square.

Sa Pobla

From Muro, it's just 4km northwest to the dusty little agricultural town of **Sa Pobla**, whose straightforward grid-iron of old streets is at its prettiest in the main square, the Plaça Constitució, which is also the site of a busy Sunday-morning market.

Also of some mild interest is Can Planes, c/Antoni Maura 6, a late nineteenth-century *Modernista* mansion that has been turned into a cultural centre incorporating a contemporary art gallery and toy museum, the **Museu d'Art Contemporani i Jugeta Antigua** (Tues–Sat 10am–1.30pm & 4–7.30pm, Sun 10am–1.30pm; €3). The mansion is poorly signed and can be hard to find – it's located at the north end of c/Antoni Maura (which runs north–south across the west side of the town centre), close to its intersection with Carretera Inca, the main road to Inca. The gallery's permanent collection features the work of Mallorcan and foreign artists resident on the island since the 1970s, and there's an ambitious programme of temporary exhibitions too. Upstairs, the toy museum holds an assortment of nineteenth- and early to mid-twentieth-century toys and games – some four thousand exhibits in all, from miniature rocking horses and carousels to baffling board games.

Accommodation

Ermita de Nostra Senyora del Puig

Puig Maria, Pollença ☏971 184132.
Several of the original monks'
cells here have been renovated
to provide simple rooms
sleeping between two and six
guests with shared facilities.
There's a refectory, but the
food is only average. Most
guests turn up on spec: to be
sure of a room, book ahead.
Be warned that the trek up to
the monastery is a real lung-
wrencher and note also that it
can get cold and windy up here
at night, even in the summer.
The Puig Maria is on the edge
of Pollença; for a description of
the former monastery, see p.116.
Doubles €20.

Hostal Bahía

Passeig Voramar 31, Port de Pollença
☏971 866562, ⓦwww.hoposa.es. In
a lovely location a few minutes'
walk north of the marina along
the pedestrianized part of the
seafront, this pleasant, unassuming
hostal offers thirty rooms in one
of the port's older villas. Closed
Nov–March. €80, a little more
for a sea view.

Hostatgeria Ermita de la Victòria

Ermita de la Victòria, near Alcúdia
☏971 549912, ⓦwww.lavictoriahotel
.com. The church at the
Ermita de la Victòria remains
unchanged (see p.120), but
the old monastic quarters
behind and above it have been
imaginatively converted into a
charming *hostal*. This has twelve
en-suite guest rooms decorated
in a suitably frugal, but highly
buffed and polished style.
Highly recommended and a
snip at €70.

Hotel Can Llenaire

Carretera Llenaire ☏971 535251,
ⓦwww.hotelllenaire.com. This
imposing Mallorcan manor
house sits on the brow of a hill
with wide views over the Badia
de Pollença, the mountains
glinting in the distance. The
owner still operates a farm
here, with sheep grazing and
groves of almond and olive
trees, but the house itself has
been turned into a charming
hotel with most of the original
architectural features, dating
back to the eighteenth century,
sympathetically renovated.
There are just eleven rooms,
each decked out in period style.
The hotel is clearly signposted
down a country lane from the
main coastal road just east of the
centre of Port de Pollença. €210.

Hotel Es Convent

c/Progrés 6, Alcúdia ☏971 548716,
ⓦwww.esconvent.com. Right
in the centre of Alcúdia, this
charming hotel occupies an
exquisitely restored medieval
building, all beamed ceilings,
bare stone walls and arches.
Modern additions are
minimalist, with lots of whites
and creams, and this applies in
equal measure to the four guest
bedrooms. The restaurant here
is excellent too, featuring local
ingredients and dishes. €90.

Hotel Formentor

Platja de Formentor ☏971 899101,
ⓦwww.hotelformentor.net. Opened
in 1930, this grand old hotel
– in its heyday the island's best
– lies low against a forested
hillside, its *hacienda*-style
architecture enhanced by
Neoclassical and Art Deco
features and exquisite terraced
gardens. The place was once
the haunt of the rich and
fashionable – Charlie Chaplin

and F. Scott Fitzgerald both stayed here – and although its socialite days are long gone, the hotel preserves an air of understated elegance. It has every facility, and dinner is served on an outside terrace perfumed by the flowers of the gardens; breakfast is taken on the splendid upper-floor loggia with spectacular views over the bay. The rooms are not quite as grand as you might expect, but are still charming. Stay here if you can afford it; there's a good chance of a vacant room, even in high season. €250.

Hotel Juma

Plaça Major 9, Pollença ☎971 535002, ⓦwww.hoteljuma.com. Characterful three-star hotel occupying a smart and tastefully converted old stone merchant's house in the heart of the old town – and above a café. The guest rooms are tidily furnished in brisk modern style with a/c. Rooms overlooking the square cost a few euros extra. €110.

Hotel Sis Pins

Passeig Anglada Camarasa 77, Port de Pollença ☎971 86 70 50 ⓦwww.flyglobespan.com. Medium-sized, three-star hotel occupying a handsome whitewashed and balconied villa on the pedestrianized part of the waterfront. Closed Nov–March. €125.

Hotel Son Sant Jordi

c/Sant Jordi 29, Pollença ☎971 530389, ⓦwww.hotelsonsantjordi.com. This well-appointed hotel occupies an attractively converted old stone merchant's house in the centre of Pollença. The guest rooms are decorated in an attractive modern style in keeping with their surroundings. All rooms have a/c, satellite TV,

minibar and safe, and there's a large garden out back with a sizeable pool. €160.

Monestir de Nostra Senyora de Lluc

Lluc ☎971 871525, ⓔinfo@lluc.net. At Lluc monastery, room rental is highly organized, with simple, self-contained cells and apartments. In summer, phone ahead if you want to be sure of space, at other times simply book at the monastery's information office on arrival. There's an 11pm curfew, except for the apartments, which have their own separate entrance. From €18 per person.

Posada de Lluc

c/Roser Vell 11, Pollença ☎971 535220, ⓦwww.posadalluc.com. Small and very comfortable hotel in attractively restored old stone townhouse in the centre of Pollença. The monks from Lluc monastery (see p.110) used to lodge here when they popped into town to pick up supplies, and many of the original features have been kept, most notably the deep stone arches. There's a small outside pool and each of the guest rooms has been kitted out in an appropriate modern version of period style. €120.

Restaurants

Café-Bar Juma

Plaça Major 9, Pollença ☎971 535002. Daily 10am–midnight. Good range of tasty *tapas* sold in the brisk, modern bar of the *Hotel Juma*. Rapid-fire service and reasonable prices – a standard portion of *tapas* costs about €5. The outside terrace overlooking the main square is especially enticing.

Café La Balada del Agua del Mar

Passeig Voramar 5, Port de Pollença ☎971 864276. Lovely, little beachside café-restaurant occupying an old villa whose terrace is shaded by an ancient fig tree. Good salads and seafood. Mains €11–17.

Restaurant Cantonet

c/Monti-Sion 20, Pollença ☎971 530429. Daily except Tues 7–11pm; closed Nov–Jan. This fashionable restaurant just north of Plaça Major offers top-notch international/Italian cuisine from a limited menu with main courses starting from as little as €11. In the summer, you can eat out on the terrace of the large church next door.

Restaurant Clivia

Avgda Pollentia 5, Pollença ☎971 533635. Daily except Wed 1–3pm & 7-10pm. Very hospitable restaurant, a long-time expatriate favourite, offering an excellent range of Spanish dishes – try the squid in ink. If you choose fish, then the waiter brings the uncooked version to the table so you can inspect it, which is really rather refreshing. The decor is traditional Spanish and attracts an older clientele. Mains €15–20.

Restaurant Il Giardino

Plaça Major 11, Pollença ☎971 534302. Daily from 7pm; closed Nov to mid-March. Arguably the best restaurant in town, this smart bistro-style place offers a superb range of Italian dishes from about €14, all prepared with vim and gusto and featuring the best of local ingredients. To be sure of a seat on the terrace – where you will probably want to eat – either come early or book ahead. Great house wines too.

Restaurant Little Italy

Passeig Voramar 57, Port de Pollença ☎971 866749. Amenable and very popular restaurant, where the pizzas (from €10) are large, authentically Italian and very, *very* good.

Restaurant Mirador de la Victòria

Beside the Ermita de la Victòria, near Alcúdia ☎971 547173. Closed Mon. Laid-back, informal restaurant occupying a magnificent location with sweeping sea views from its expansive terrace. The food is first-rate too; guinea fowl and chicken are two specialities. Very reasonable prices.

Restaurant Stay

Moll Nou jetty, Port de Pollença ☎971 864013. Daily noon–10.30pm. Recently refitted, this long-established restaurant, with its crisp modern decor and attentive service, is renowned for the quality of its seafood – though the main courses tend towards the minimal. Prices are a bit above average, but well

▼ RESTAURANT IS GIARDINO

▲ RESTAURANT MIRADOR DE LA VICTÒRIA

worth it for the setting out on the pier; superb desserts and great wine list too. It's a very popular spot, so reservations are pretty much essential. Mains from €22.

Shopping

Alcúdia market

Alcúdia. Tues & Sun from 8am. Fantastically popular open-air market, whose stalls sprawl over the east side of the town centre from Plaça Carles V to the main square, Plaça Constitució. Everything is here, from the worst of tourist tat to designer clothes and fresh fruit and veg.

Bennassar Galleries

Plaça Major 6, Pollença ☎971 533514. Thurs–Sat 10am–1pm & 5–9pm & Sun 11am–1.30pm. Pollença has established something of a reputation for its fine-art galleries and this is perhaps the most inventive, featuring contemporary artists of various skills and techniques.

Ensenat

c/Alcúdia 11, Pollença. Mon–Fri 10am–1.30pm & 5–7.30pm, Sat 10am–1pm. Excellent wine and speciality food shop stocked with all things *Mallorquín*, from hams and sausages to olives and almonds.

Southern Mallorca

Southern Mallorca mostly consists of the island's central plain, Es Pla, a fertile tract bounded by the Serres de Llevant, the hilly range that shadows the east coast. Before the tourist boom of the 1960s, when the developers bypassed the plain to focus on the coast, Es Pla largely defined Mallorca. The majority of the island's inhabitants lived here and it produced enough food to meet almost every domestic requirement. Even today you can still get the full flavour of an older, agricultural Mallorca, whose softly hued landscapes are patterned with country towns of low, whitewashed houses. Obvious targets include Sineu, which has a particularly imposing parish church, and Petra, with its clutch of sights celebrating the life of the eighteenth-century Franciscan monk and explorer Junípero Serra. Other places worth searching out are the Gordiola Glassworks, Els Calderers, a country house illustrating *hacienda* life in the nineteenth century, and the monastery perched on the summit of Puig Randa. In the Serres de Llevant, aim for Artà's hilltop shrine, the prehistoric ruins of Ses Paisses, the Santuari de Sant Salvador monastery and the medieval castle at Capdepera.

Most of the picturesque coves and tiny fishing villages of the **east coast** have been swallowed up within a string of mega-resorts, but three have managed to retain much of their original charm: **Cala Rajada**, a lively holiday spot bordered by fine beaches and a beautiful pine-shrouded coastline, **Cala Figuera**, which surrounds a lovely, steep-sided cove, and **Porto Petro**. Different again are the old and amenable port of **Porto Cristo** and tiny **Cala Mondragó**, where a slice of coast has been belatedly protected by the creation of a park. The east coast also holds the cave systems of **Coves d'Artà** and **Coves del Drac**, famous for their dramatic stalactites and stalagmites. On the south coast, the hills and coves give way to sparse flatlands and the only star turn is the port-cum-resort of **Colònia de Sant Jordi**, from where summer boat trips leave for the scrubby remoteness of fauna-rich **Cabrera island**.

The Gordiola Glassworks

Ctra Palma–Manacor, Km 19. June–Sept Mon–Sat 9am–8pm, Sun 9am–1.30pm; Oct–May Mon–Sat 9am–6.30pm, Sun 9am–1.30pm; free. Heading east from Palma on the MA-15, it's about 19km to the roadside **Can Gordiola glassworks**, which occupies a conspicuous castle-like building, whose crenellated walls and clumsy loggias date from the

Transport and accommodation

Given the difficulty of finding a room in the coastal package resorts on spec and the general dearth of **accommodation** in the interior, advance reservations are a good idea – and pretty much essential in the height of the season. Potential bases, each of which has a healthy supply of non-package hotels and *hostals*, include Artà, Cala Rajada and Colònia de Sant Jordi. In addition, three of the region's former **monasteries** offer simple, inexpensive lodgings, and usually have space at any time of year. These are the Santuari de Nostra Senyora de Cura, on Puig Randa near Algaida; the Ermita de Nostra Senyora de Bonany, near Petra; and the Santuari de Sant Salvador outside Felanitx.

Direct **buses** link Palma with almost every resort and town in the region, but services between the towns of Es Pla and along the east coast are patchy. More positively, there are fast and frequent **trains** east from Palma to Inca, Sineu, Petra and Manacor with **connecting bus services** leaving Inca and Manacor train stations for surrounding towns and villages.

1960s. Don't be put off by its appearance, however, or by the herd of tourist coaches parked outside, for here you can watch highly skilled **glassblowers** in action, practising their precise art in a gloomy hall designed to resemble a medieval church and illuminated by glowing furnaces. Staff are usually on hand to explain the techniques involved – the fusion of silica, soda and lime at a temperature of 1100°C – though this is really part of a public-relations exercise intended to push

you towards the adjacent gift shops (see p.152), which hold a massive assortment of glass and ceramic items.

The gift shops are one thing, but the museum, on the top floor, is quite another. The owners of the glassworks, the Gordiola family, have been in business in Mallorca since the early eighteenth century and they have accumulated an extraordinary collection of glassware, now displayed in fifty-odd cabinets. Of the pieces on display, some of the

▼ GORDIOLA GLASSWORKS

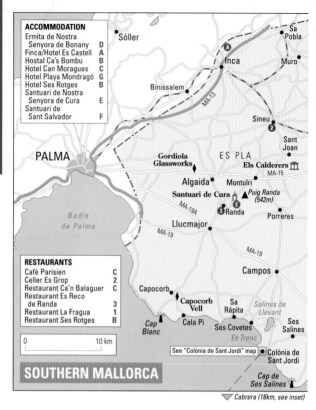

SOUTHERN MALLORCA

ACCOMMODATION
Ermita de Nostra
  Senyora de Bonany   D
Finca/Hotel Es Castell   A
Hostal Ca's Bombu   B
Hotel Can Moragues   C
Hotel Playa Mondragó   G
Hotel Ses Rotges   B
Santuari de Nostra
  Senyora de Cura   E
Santuari de
  Sant Salvador   F

RESTAURANTS
Café Parisien   C
Celler Es Grop   2
Restaurant Ca'n Balaguer C
Restaurant Es Reco
  de Randa   3
Restaurant La Fragua   1
Restaurant Ses Rotges   B

0   10 km

Cabrera (18km, see inset)

most interesting are the earliest
Gordiola work, green-coloured
jugs of a frothy consistency,
where both the shade and
the trapped air bubbles were
unwanted – only later did
improved technology allow
for colour clarification and the
removal of the last air bubbles.
Amongst later work, kitchen-
and tableware predominate
– bottles, vases, jugs and glasses
in a variety of shades, of
which green remains the most
distinctive. The Gordiola pieces
are, however, but a fraction
of the collection, with other
cabinets featuring pieces from

every corner of the globe.
Unfortunately the labelling is
abysmal and so, to make much
sense of what you see, you'll
need to invest in a guidebook
(€6) on sale at the gift shops.

Algaida and Puig Randa

Algaida is typical of the small
agricultural towns that sprinkle
Mallorca's central plain – low,
whitewashed houses fanning
out from an old Gothic-
Baroque church. There's nothing
remarkable about the place, but
if you're travelling the MA-15
you'll need to pass through here
to reach the five-kilometre-long

byroad that clambers to the top of **Puig Randa**, at 542 metres the highest of a slim band of hills lying to the north of Llucmajor.

The top of Puig Randa is flat enough to accommodate a substantial walled complex, the **Santuari de Nostra Senyora de Cura** (Hermitage of Our Lady of Cura). Entry is through a seventeenth-century portal, but most of the buildings beyond are plain and modern, the work of the present incumbents, Franciscan monks who arrived in 1913 after the site had lain abandoned for decades. The oldest surviving

building is the quaintly gabled chapel, a homely and familiar affair partly dating from the 1660s, but you'll soon be moving on to either the terrace café, which offers average food and superb views, or the information office, where you can fix yourself up with a room.

There are also two other, less significant sanctuaries on the lower slopes of Puig Randa. Heading back down the hill, it's a couple of kilometres to the easily missable sharp left turn for the **Santuari de Sant Honorat**, which comprises a tiny church and

▲ SANTUARI DE NOSTRA SENYORA DE CURA

a few conventual buildings of medieval provenance.

Back on the main summit road, a further 1.2km down the hill, is the more appealing third and final monastery, the **Santuari de Gràcia**, which is approached through a signposted gateway on the left. Founded in the fifteenth century, the whitewashed walls of this tiny sanctuary are tucked underneath a severe cliff face, which throngs with nesting birds, and there are wide views over Es Pla's rolling farmland.

Montuïri

Montuïri is a gentle sweep of pastel-shaded stone houses on a low hill immediately north of the main MA-15. In the heart of the town, it's worth taking a peek at the largely Gothic church of **Sant Bartomeu**, an imposing pile plonked next to the small main square and the proud possessor of several handsome Baroque altarpieces.

The next place of interest on the MA-15 east of Montuïri is the fascinating old country house of Els Calderers (see p.134), but the town is also a convenient starting point for the short detour north along country roads to Sineu and Petra (see below).

Sineu

Sineu is undoubtedly the most interesting of the ancient agricultural towns of the central plain. Glued to a hill at the geographical centre of the island, the town had obvious strategic advantages for the independent kings of fourteenth-century Mallorca. Jaume II built a royal palace here; his asthmatic successor Sancho came to take the upland air in Sineu; and the last of the dynasty, Jaume III, slept here the night before he was defeated and killed at the battle of Llucmajor by Pedro of Aragón.

The new Aragonese monarchs had no need of the Sineu palace, which disappeared long ago, but former pretensions survive in the massive stone facade of **Nostra Senyora de los Angeles**, the grandest parish church on the island. Built in the thirteenth century,

▼ SINEU

the church was extensively remodelled three hundred years later, but the majestic simplicity of the original Gothic design is still plain to see. At the side, a single-span arch connects with the colossal free-standing bell tower, and at the front, at the top of the steps, a big, modern and aggressive statue of a winged lion – the emblem of the town's patron, St Mark – stands guard, courtesy of Franco's cronies.

Beside the church is the unassuming main square, **Sa Plaça**, where you'll find a couple of traditional Mallorcan bar-restaurants, which are packed to the gunnels on Wednesdays, when the town fizzes with Mallorca's biggest fresh produce and livestock markets.

Inca

Poor old **Inca**, Mallorca's third city, has long had a bad press as an industrial eyesore. In medieval times, one of the few ways to keep out of the clutches of the island's landowners was to practise a craft and then join the appropriate guild. As early as the fifteenth century, Inca had attracted enough **shoemakers** to become the centre of a flourishing shoemaking industry – and so it remains today with Camper's HQ firmly ensconced here. This may not sound too enticing, but the town centre has recently been spruced up and the walk across its pedestrianized core, from the train station in the west to Plaça Orient in the east, is an agreeable way to spend an hour or so. Along the way, you'll spy a scattering of immaculate *Modernista* buildings and the town's main church, Santa Maria la Major, an imposing sandstone pile with all sorts of Baroque flourishes.

Petra

Nothing very exciting happens in **Petra** but it was the birthplace of **Junípero Serra**, the eighteenth-century Franciscan friar who played an important role in the settlement of Spanish North America. Serra's missionary endeavours began in 1749 when he landed at Veracruz on the Gulf of Mexico. For eighteen years Serra thrashed around the remoter parts of Mexico until, entirely by chance, political machinations back in Europe saved him from obscurity. In 1768, Carlos III claimed the west coast of the North American continent for Spain and, to substantiate his claim, dispatched a small expeditionary force of soldiers and monks north; Serra led the priests. The walk from Mexico City to California was pretty daunting, but almost all the force survived to reach the Pacific Ocean somewhere near the present US–Mexico border in early 1769. Over the next decade, Serra and his small party of priests set about converting the Native Americans of coastal California to the Catholic faith, and established a string of nine missions along the Pacific coast, including San Diego, Los Angeles and San Francisco. Pope John Paul II beatified Serra in 1988.

▼ JUNÍPERO SERRA HOUSE, PETRA

Petra makes a reasonable hand of its connection with Serra. In the upper part of town, on c/Major, is the chunky church of **Sant Bernat**, beside which – down a narrow side street – lies a modest sequence of *majolica* panels honouring Serra's life and missionary work. This simple tribute is backed up by a self-effacing **museum** (Mon–Fri 9am–7pm; donation requested) in a pleasant old house at the end of this same side street, with several rooms devoted to Serra's cult. Two doors up the street, at no. 6, is the humble whitewashed stone and brick house where he was born. The museum and house are sometimes locked, but there should be instructions posted outside explaining how to contact the custodian.

Ermita de Nostra Senyora de Bonany

The hilltop **Ermita de Nostra Senyora de Bonany**, some 5km southwest of Petra, offers extensive views over Es Pla. To get there, take the Felanitx road out of Petra and look out for the sign on the edge of the village. The monastery is at the end of a bumpy, four-kilometre country lane, and takes its name from events in 1609 when desperate locals gathered here at the chapel to pray for rain. Shortly afterwards, the drought broke and the ensuing harvest was a good one – hence *bon any* ("good year"). The prettiest feature of the complex is the chapel, which is approached along an avenue of cypress and palm trees and comes complete with a rose window, twin towers and a little cupola. The monastery's conspicuous stone cross was erected in honour of Junípero Serra, who left here

bound for the Americas in 1749. There are also five simple double rooms for rent here (see p.149).

Els Calderers

Daily: April–Oct 10am–6pm; Nov–March 10am–5pm; €10. Dating mostly from the eighteenth century, **Els Calderers** is a charming country house that bears witness to the wealth and influence once enjoyed by the island's landed gentry – in this case the Veri family. It's tucked away at the end of a country lane 2km north of – and clearly signposted from – the MA-15.

The **house** was the focus of a large estate, which produced a mixed bag of agricultural produce: the main cash crop was originally grapes, though this changed in the 1870s when phylloxera, a greenfly-like aphid, destroyed Mallorca's (and most of Europe's) vineyards. The Veris switched to cereals, and at the beginning of the twentieth century were at the forefront of efforts to modernize Mallorcan agriculture. The entrance to the house, flanked by a pair of crumpled-looking lions, leads to a sequence of handsome rooms surrounding a cool courtyard. All are kitted out with antique furniture, *objets d'art* and family portraits, and each has a clearly defined function, from the dainty music room to the hunting room, with assorted stuffed animal heads, and the master's office, with big armchairs and a much-polished desk. You can also see the family's tiny **chapel** and there's more religious material upstairs in the assorted prints that line the walls. Attached to, but separate from, the family house are the living quarters of the *amo* (farm manager), the barn and the farmworkers'

▲ ARTÀ

kitchen and eating area. To complete your visit, take a stroll round the **animal pens**, which hold breeds traditionally used on Mallorcan farms, and pop into the **café**, where they serve traditional island snacks – the *pa amb oli* (bread rubbed with olive oil) with ham and cheese is delicious.

Manacor

Hometown of the tennis star Rafael Nadal, industrial **Manacor** declares its business long before you arrive, with vast roadside hoardings promoting its furniture, wrought-iron and artificial pearl factories. On the strength of these, the city has risen to become Mallorca's second urban centre, much smaller than Palma, but large enough to have spawned unappetising suburbs on all sides. More positively, Manacor's old centre has been attractively restored, the prime target here being the **Església Nostra Senyora Verge dels Dolors** (daily 8.30am–12.30pm & 5.30–8pm; free), a sprawling stone church built on the site of the Moors' main mosque in the thirteenth century, though what you see today is Neo-Gothic. The church abuts **Plaça Rector Rubí**, a busy square

that is home to the *Palau Café* (closed Sun), at no. 8, where you can sample a local speciality, spicy pork sausage made from black pig (*sobrasada de cerdo negro*). From the square, it's a short walk northwest to Manacor's other principal sight, the **Convent de Sant Vicenç Ferrer** (Mon–Fri 8am–2pm & 5–8pm; free), on Plaça Convent, a classically Baroque complex dating from the late sixteenth century.

Artà

The top end of the **Serres de Llevant** range bunches up to fill out Mallorca's eastern corner, providing a dramatic backdrop to **Artà**, an ancient hill town of sun-bleached roofs clustered beneath a castellated chapel-shrine. It's a delightful scene, though at close quarters the town is something of an anticlimax with the cobweb of cramped and twisted alleys not quite matching the setting. That said, the ten-minute trek up to the **Santuari de Sant Salvador**, the panoramic shrine at the top of Artà, is a must. It's almost impossible to get lost, just keep going upwards: follow c/Ciutat as it slices across the edge of Plaça Conqueridor, and then head straight on up to Plaça Espanya, a leafy little piazza that is home to the town hall. Beyond, a short stroll through streets of gently decaying mansions brings you to the gargantuan parish church of Sant Salvador. From this unremarkable pile, steep stone steps and cypress trees lead up the Via Crucis (Way of the Cross) to the *santuari*, which, in its present form, dates from the early nineteenth century, though the hilltop has been a place of pilgrimage for much longer. The interior of the present chapel is hardly awe-inspiring – the paintings are mediocre and the curious statue of Jesus behind the altar has him smiling as if he has lost his mental marbles – but the views are exquisite, with the picturesque town below and Es Pla stretching away to distant hills.

Ses Paisses

April–Oct daily 10am–12.30pm & 2.30–6.30pm; Nov–March Mon–Sat 9am–1pm & 2.30–5pm; €1.50.
Tucked away in a grove of olive, carob and holm-oak trees, the elegiacally rustic remains of the Talayotic village of **Ses Paisses** are about 1km south of Artà. To get there, walk to the bottom of c/Ciutat, turn left along the main through-road and watch for the signposted and well-surfaced country lane on the right. A clear footpath explores every nook and cranny of the site, and its numbered markers are thoroughly explained in the English-language guidebook available at the entrance (€2).

The village is entered through a monolithic gateway, whose heavyweight jambs and lintel interrupt the Cyclopean walls that still encircle the site. These outer remains date from the second phase of the Talayotic culture (c.1000–800 BC), when the emphasis was on consolidation and defence; in places, the walls still stand at their original size, around 3.5m high and 3m thick. Beside the gate, there's also a modern plinth erected in honour of Miquel Llobera, a local writer who penned romantic verses about the place.

Beyond the gateway, the central *talayot* is from the first Talayotic phase (c.1300–1000 BC), its shattered ruins flanked by the foundations of several rooms of later date and uncertain purpose. Experts believe the horseshoe-shaped room was used, at least towards the end of the Talayotic period, for cremations, whilst the three rectangular rooms were probably living quarters. In the rooms, archeologists discovered various items such as iron objects and ceramics imported from elsewhere in the Mediterranean. Some of them were perhaps brought back from the Punic Wars (264–146 BC) by mercenaries – the skills of Balearic stone-slingers were highly prized by the Carthaginians, and it's known that several hundred accompanied Hannibal and his elephants over the Alps in 218 BC.

The Ermita de Betlem

Hidden away in the hills 10km northwest of Artà, the **Ermita de Betlem** is a remote and minuscule hermitage founded in 1805. In itself, the *ermita* is not a major pull, but the scenery hereabouts is handsome indeed. The road to the *ermita* begins on the north side of Artà beyond Plaça Espanya, but the start is poorly signed and tricky to find: aim for c/Figueretes, go past the *Hotel Sant Salvador* and then follow the signs. The road's rough surface and snaking course also make for a difficult drive, so an alternative is to **walk** – reckon on five or six hours for the return trip. The first portion is an easy stroll up along the wooded valley of the **Torrent des Cocons**, but then – after about 3km – the road squeezes through the narrowest of defiles, with the hills rising steeply on either side. Beyond, the road begins to climb into the hills of the Serra de Llevant – here the **Massís d'Artà** – until, some 3km after the defile, a signposted turn signals the start of the strenuous part of the journey. Here, the track wriggles for 4km up and down the steep hillside before finally reaching the *ermita* at the end of a cypress-lined path.

Amongst the huddle of old stone buildings that comprises the *ermita*, the **church** is perhaps the most interesting structure, its ponderous bulk holding crude religious paintings on the walls and a poor-quality fresco on the ceiling. The *ermita*'s only facility is a small shop (with uncertain opening hours) that sells religious trinkets and postcards, but there's more than enough compensation in the panoramic views down along the coast and across the Badia d'Alcúdia.

Cala Rajada

Awash with cafés, bars and hotels, vibrant **Cala Rajada** lies on the southerly side of a stubby headland in the northeast corner of Mallorca. The resort was once a fishing village, but there's little evidence of this today, and the harbour is now packed with cruise and pleasure boats. Otherwise, the pocket-sized centre is no more than an unassuming patchwork of low-rise modern buildings, but it's all very neat and trim and there's compensation nearby in the wild and rocky coastline, where pine-clad hills shelter a series of delightful beaches.

From the harbour, walkways extend along the headland's south coast. To the southwest, past the busiest part of town, it takes about ten to fifteen minutes to stroll round to **Platja Son Moll**, a slender arc of sand overlooked by Goliath-like hotels. More rewarding is the ten-minute stroll east from the harbour to **Cala Gat,** a narrow cove beach tucked tight up against the steep, wooded coastline. The beach is far from undiscovered – there's a beach bar and at times it gets decidedly crowded – but it's an attractive spot all the same.

▼ CALA AGULLA BEACH, CALA RAJADA

Up above the footpath to Cala Gat you can glimpse the gardens of the Palau Joan March, a lavish mansion built in 1916 for the eponymous tobacco baron (see p.56). Beyond the gardens, continuing east along c/Elíonor Servera, the road twists steeply up through the pine woods to reach, after about 1km, the bony headlands and lighthouse of the **Cap de Capdepera**, Mallorca's most easterly point.

On the northern side of Cala Rajada, c/L'Agulla crosses the promontory to hit the north coast at **Platja Cala Agulla**. The approach road, some 2km of tourist tackiness, is of little appeal, but the beach, a vast curve of bright golden sand, is big enough to accommodate hundreds of bronzing pectorals with plenty of space to spare. The further you walk – and there are signed and shaded footpaths through the pine woods to assist you – the more isolation you'll get.

Capdepera

Spied across the valley from the west or south, the crenellated walls dominating **Capdepera**, a tiny village 8km east of Artà

and 3km west of Cala Rajada, look too pristine to be true. Yet the triangular fortifications are genuine enough, built in the fourteenth century by the Mallorcan King Sancho to protect the coast from pirates. The village, snuggled below the walls, contains a pleasant medley of old houses, its slender main square, Plaça de L'Orient, acting as a prelude to the steep steps up to the Castell de Capdepera (daily: April–Oct 9am–8pm; Nov–March 10am–5pm; €3). The steps are the most pleasant way to reach the castle, but you can also follow the signs and drive up narrow c/Major. Flowering cactuses give the fortress a special allure in late May and June, but it's a beguiling place at any time, with over 400m of walls equipped with a parapet walkway and sheltering neat terraced gardens. At the top of the fortress, **Nostra Senyora de la Esperança** (Our Lady of Good Hope) is the quaintest of Gothic churches: its aisle-less, vaulted frame is furnished with outside steps leading up, behind the bell gable, to a flat roof, from where the views are simply superb.

▼ CAPDEPERA

The Coves d'Artà

Tours of the caves run every half-hour daily: May–Oct 10am–6pm; Nov–April 10am–5pm; €9; ⊛www.cuevasdearta .com. The succession of coves, caves and beaches notching the Mallorcan seashore between Cala Rajada and Cala Millor begins promisingly with the memorable **Coves d'Artà** (often signposted in Castilian as "Cuevas de Artà"), reached along the first turning off the main coastal road south of Capdepera.

This is the pick of the numerous cave systems of eastern Mallorca, its sequence of cavernous chambers, studded with stalagmites and stalactites, extending 450m into the rock. Artificial lighting exaggerates the bizarre shapes of the caverns and their accretions, especially in the **Hall of Flags**, where stalactites up to 50m long hang in the shape of partly unfurled flags. Exiting the caves, you're greeted with a stunning view, courtesy of a majestic stairway straight out of a horror movie that leads down from the yawning hole, beckoning like the mouth of hell high in the cliffs above the bay.

The caves have had a chequered history. During the Reconquista, a thousand Moorish refugees from Artà were literally smoked out of the caves to be slaughtered by Catalan soldiers waiting outside. In the nineteenth century, touring the caves for their scientific interest became fashionable amongst the rich and famous – Jules Verne was particularly impressed – and visits now feature prominently on many a package-tour itinerary. Allow about an hour for the visit – more if there's a queue, as there sometimes is.

Cala Millor

The well-heeled villas of **Costa dels Pins** comprise the most northerly and prosperous portion of a gigantic resort conurbation centred on **Cala Bona** and **Cala Millor**. This is development gone quite mad, a swathe of apartment buildings, sky-rise hotels and villa-villages overwhelming the contours of the coast as far as the eye can see. The only redeeming feature – and the reason for all this frantic construction in the first place – is the beach, a magnificent two-kilometre stretch of sand fringed by what remains of the old pine woods. A headland away there are yet more acres of concrete and glass at **Sa Coma** and **S'Illot**. To avoid this visual assault, stay on the main coastal road, which runs just inland from the resorts, cutting a rustic route through vineyards and almond groves before reaching the multicoloured billboards, which announce the cave systems of Porto Cristo.

Porto Cristo

Although **Porto Cristo** prospered in the early days of the tourist boom, sprouting a string of hotels and *hostals*, it's fared badly since mega-resorts such as Cala Millor and Cala d'Or were constructed nearby: don't be deceived by the jam of tourist buses clogging the town's streets on their way to the nearby Coves del Drac (see p.141) – few of their occupants will actually be staying here. Porto Cristo has benefited from a recent revamp, but it's still a modest sort of place with a small sliver of beach, which is good enough for sunbathing, though the swimming is poor; it is tucked inside the harbour,

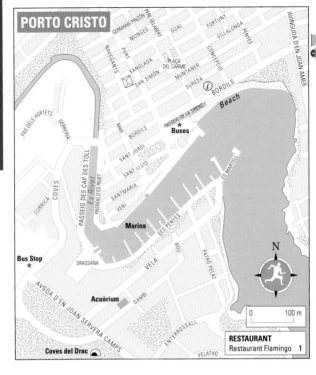

PORTO CRISTO

RESTAURANT
Restaurant Flamingo 1

a narrow V-shaped channel entered between a pair of rocky promontories that is one of the most sheltered ports on Mallorca's east coast.

Porto Cristo's origins are uncertain, but it was definitely in existence by the thirteenth century, when it served as the fishing harbour and seaport of the inland town of Manacor. Nothing remains of the medieval settlement, however, and today the centre, which climbs the hill behind the harbour, consists of high-sided terraced buildings mostly dating from the late nineteenth and early twentieth centuries. In August 1936, Porto Cristo was the site of a **Republican landing** in an attempt to capture the island from Franco's Falangists. The campaign was a fiasco: the Republicans disembarked over seven thousand men and quickly established a long and deep bridgehead, but their commanders, completely surprised by their initial success, quite literally didn't know what to do next. The Nationalists did: they counterattacked and, supported by the Italian air force, soon had the Republicans dashing back to the coast. Barcelona radio put on a brave face, announcing, "The heroic Catalan columns have returned from Mallorca after a magnificent action. Not a single man suffered from the effects of the embarkation."

Coves del Drac

Hour-long guided tours daily: April–Oct 10am–5pm; Nov–March 10.30am–4.30pm; €9.50, no cards; ⓦwww.cuevasdeldrac.com. Porto Cristo's pride and joy, the **Coves del Drac** (often signposted in Castilian "Cuevas del Drach"), is located across the Es Rivet river, about fifteen minutes' walk south of the town centre along the coastal road. Locals had known of the "Dragon's Caves" for hundreds of years, but it was the Austrian archduke Ludwig Salvator (see p.96) who recruited French geologists to explore and map them in 1896. The French discovered four huge chambers that penetrated the coast's limestone cliffs for a distance of around 2km. In the last cavern they found one of the largest subterranean lakes in the world, some 177m long, 40m wide and 30m deep. Thoroughly commercialized, the present complex accommodates a giant car park, ticket office and restaurant, behind which lurk the gardens that lead to the flight of steps down to the caves. You may come to know each step well, as you can wait in line for ages, especially at the weekend.

Inside, the myriad concretions of calcium carbonate, formed by the dissolution of the soft limestone by rainwater, are shrewdly illuminated. Shunting you through the hour-long, multilingual tour, the guides invite you to gawp and gush at formations such as "the Buddha" and "the Pagoda", as well as magnificent icicle-like stalactites, some of which are snowy white, others picking up hints of orange and red from the rocks they hang off. The *tour de force* is the larger of the two subterranean lakes, whose translucent waters flicker with reflected colours, the effects enhanced by a small group of musicians drifting by in boats; performances usually begin on the hour.

From the cave complex, it's a short walk across the car park to the well-stocked **Acuàrium** (daily: April–Oct 9.30am–5pm; Nov–March 11am–3pm; €5). Mediterranean creatures lurk on the upper floor, while displays of international ocean life can be found below, where the glass tanks magnify such exotic horrors as electric eels, piranhas and stinging fish.

Coves d'es Hams

Guided tours every half-hour: daily April–Oct 10am–5pm; Nov–March 10.45am–noon & 2–3.30pm; €10; ⓦwww.cuevas-hams.com. The **Coves d'es Hams** (or "Cuevas del Hams" in Castilian), situated 2km west of Porto Cristo on the road to Manacor, are not nearly as well known as their subterranean neighbour, the Coves del Drac, but a visit follows the same format. Guides escort their charges through a sequence of caverns lit to emphasize the beauty of the accumulated stalagmites, and stalactites and the whole caboodle culminates with musicians playing from boats on an underground lake.

Felanitx

The town of **Felanitx** is an industrious place, producing wine, ceramics and pearls, and, although hardly beautiful, it does have more than a modicum of charm, its tangle of narrow streets lined by handsome old houses mostly dating from the eighteenth and nineteenth centuries. The finest building is the church of **Sant Miquel**, whose mighty, soaring honey-gold facade boasts a dramatic statue of St Michael, shown triumphant with a cringing devil at his feet. The church overlooks one of the town's main squares, **Plaça Sa Font**, where, in an unusual arrangement, a wide and really rather grand flight of stone steps digs down below street level to reach **Font de Santa Margalida**, once the municipal well and now a water fountain.

The church stands on a hillock and its easterly supporting wall shadows **c/Major**. Everything looks secure today, but in 1844 the wall collapsed, killing over four hundred people in the worst disaster to hit the town since the days of pirate attack: a **plaque** on c/Major commemorates the dead. The best time to visit Felanitx is on Sunday morning, when a lively fresh produce and craft **market** takes over much of the town centre; there's also a very good covered market, the **mercat municipal** (Tues–Sun), just behind **Sant Miquel** on c/Esglesia. In particular, look out for the capers (Catalan *tapèras*; Castilian *alcaparras*), produced locally and sold by size; the smallest are the most flavoursome, either as *nonpareilles* (up to 7mm) or *surfines* (7–8mm).

The Santuari de Sant Salvador

Within easy striking distance of Felanitx is one of the more scenic portions of the Serres de Llevant hills. The best and most obvious target here is the **Santuari de Sant Salvador**, whose assorted buildings stretch along a slender ridge at the top of the 510-metre-high Puig de Sant Salvador. The drive to the monastery is easy enough and takes about fifteen minutes: head east out of Felanitx on the road to Porto Colom and after about 2km take the signposted, five-kilometre-long side road that weaves its way up the mountain. The *santuari* was founded in the fourteenth century in an attempt to stave off a further visitation of the Black Death, which had mauled Felanitx in 1348. It worked, but the original buildings were demolished long ago and the present structure, a strikingly handsome fortress-like complex perched on the edge of the ridge, dates from the early eighteenth century. Inside, beyond the strongly fortified gatehouse, ancient vaulted corridors lead to the **church**, which shelters a much-venerated image of the Virgin Mary. The other end of the ridge is dominated by a gargantuan **statue of Christ the King** stuck on top of a massive plinth. The statue was erected in 1934 and is visible for miles around, though it may well be the island's ugliest landmark. As compensation, the views down across Mallorca from anywhere on the ridge are simply fabulous.

Sant Salvador was the last of Mallorca's monasteries to lose its monks – the last ones moved out in the early 1990s. Thereafter, visitors were initially lodged in the old cells, but a new wing has recently been added (see p.150).

The Castell de Santueri

The custodians at the Santuari de Sant Salvador should be able to point you towards the footpath to the **Castell de Santueri**, about 4km away across the hills to the south. The route is fairly easy to follow and the going isn't difficult, although it's still advisable to have a walking map and stout shoes. The path meanders through a pretty landscape of dry-stone walls, flowering shrubs and copses of almond and carob trees, bringing you to the castle after about an hour and a half. Glued to a rocky hilltop, the battered ramparts date from the fourteenth century, though it was the Moors who built the first stronghold here. Getting inside the ruins is pot luck: sometimes you can (in which case a small entry fee is levied at the main gate), but mostly you can't. If you don't fancy the walk, you can drive to a point below the castle along a five-kilometre country lane, signed off the Felanitx–Santanyí road about 2km south of Felanitx. Curiously enough, one strong local legend insists that Christopher Columbus was conceived here in the castle, the result of a coupling between a local servant girl, one Margalida Colom, and an imprisoned baron, Prince Carl of Viana.

Cala d'Or

South along the coast from Felanitx, the pretty little fishing villages that once studded the quiet coves as far as Porto Petro have been blasted by development. The interconnected resorts that now stand in their place are a largely indistinguishable strip of whitewashed, low-rise villas, hotels, restaurants and bars, all designed in a sort of *pueblo* style. Confusingly, this long string of resorts is now usually lumped together under the title **Cala d'Or**, though technically this name in fact refers to one particular cove. To be fair, the pseudo-Andalusian style of the new resorts blends well with the ritzy *haciendas* left by a previous generation of sun-seekers. The latter are largely concentrated on the humpy little headland which separates the "real" **Cala d'Or** from its northerly neighbour, **Cala Gran**. These two fetching little coves, tucked between the cliffs and edged by narrow golden beaches, are the highlights of the area. The beaches are jam-packed throughout the season, but the swimming is perfect and the wooded coastline here is far preferable to the more concentrated development all around.

Porto Petro

Appealing **Porto Petro** rambles round a twin-pronged cove a couple of kilometres south of Cala Gran. In the last few years, it has been swallowed by the Cala d'Or conurbation, but there's no beach here, so development has been restrained. The old fishing harbour has been turned into a marina, immaculate villas dot the gentle wooded hillsides and the old centre of the village, a tiny cluster of whitewashed houses perched on the headland above the marina, has survived in good order. The main activity is to take a boat trip or promenade round the crystal-watered cove.

The Mondragó Parc Natural

Beginning about 3km south of Porto Petro, **Mondragó Parc Natural** protects a small but diverse slice of the east coast, around two thousand acres of wetland, farmland, beach, pine and scrub. The park's road signs are a tad confusing, but there are two car parks to aim for, both signposted from the MA-19 between Porto Petro and Santanyí. The better target is the **Fonts de n'Alis** car park, 100m from the tiny resort of Cala Mondragó (see below), and this can also be reached direct from Porto Petro along a country road – just follow the signs; the other car park, **S'Amarador**, is on the low-lying headland south across the cove from Cala Mondragó. The park is latticed with footpaths and country lanes, and you can pick up a (rather poor) map from the Fonts de n'Alis visitor centre (daily 9am–4pm; ☏971 181022), at the Fonts de n'Alis car park. This shows the park's four hiking trails: all are easy loops, two of forty minutes, two of thirty. Until the visitor centre sorts itself out with proper hiking maps, the only reliable reference is the billboard map displayed outside.

Cala Mondragó

Cala Mondragó is one of Mallorca's prettiest resorts. There was some development here before the creation of the park in 1990, but it's all very low key and barely disturbs the cove's beauty, with low, pine-clad cliffs framing a pair of sandy beaches beside crystal-clear waters. Predictably, the cove's "unspoilt" reputation and safe bathing acts as a magnet for sun-lovers from miles around, but you can escape the crowds by staying the night (if there's space) at the beachside *Hotel Playa Mondragó* (see p.150).

Santanyí

The crossroads town of **Santanyí** was once an important medieval stronghold guarding the island's southeastern approaches. Turkish and Berber pirates ransacked the place on several occasions, but one of the old town gates, Sa Porta, has survived along with the occasional chunk of masonry from the old city walls. Otherwise, it is Santanyí's narrow alleys, squeezed between high-sided stone houses, that are the town's main appeal, not to mention the pleasant pavement cafés edging the main square.

Cala Figuera and Cala Santanyí

Travelling southeast from Santanyí, a 5km-long byroad cuts a pretty, rustic route through to **Cala Figuera**, whose antique harbour sits beside a fjord-like inlet below the steepest of coastal cliffs. Local fishermen still land their catches and mend their nets here, but nowadays it's to the accompaniment of scores of photo-snapping tourists. Up above, the pine-covered shoreline heaves with villas, hotels and *hostals*, although the absence of high-rise buildings means the development is never overbearing. What you won't get is a beach. The nearest is 4km west at **Cala Santanyí**, a busy little resort with a medium-sized (and frequently crowded) beach at the end of a steep-sided, heavily wooded gulch. To get there, head back towards Santanyí for about 2km and follow the signs.

Cap de Ses Salines

Heading southwest from Santanyí, a fast and easy country road drifts through a landscape of old dry-stone walls, broken-down windmills, ochre-flecked farmhouses and straggling fields on its way towards Colònia de

Sant Jordi (see below). After
about 4km, you pass through
tiny Es Llombards and shortly
afterwards reach the turning
that leads the 10km down
through coastal pine woods to
the lighthouse on **Cap de Ses
Salines**, a bleak, brush-covered
headland which is Mallorca's
most southerly point. The
lighthouse itself is closed to the
public, but there are fine views
out to sea. Thekla larks and
stone curlews are often to be
seen on the cape, whilst gulls,
terns and shearwaters glide
about offshore, benefiting from
the winds which, when they're
up, can make the place well-
nigh intolerable.

▲ COLÒNIA DE SANT JORDI HARBOUR

Colònia de Sant Jordi

Altogether one of the most
appealing of Mallorca's mid-
range resorts, the wide streets
and breezy avenues of **Colònia
de Sant Jordi** pattern a
substantial and irregularly
shaped headland about 13km
west of Santanyí. The main
approach road is the Avinguda
Marquès del Palmer, at the
end of which – roughly in
the middle of the headland
– lies the principal square, the
unremarkable Plaça Constitució.
From here, c/Sa Solta and then
Avinguda Primavera lead west
to the sprawling *Hotel Marquès
del Palmer*, sitting tight against
the **Platja d'Estanys**, whose
gleaming sands curve round a
dune-edged cove.

South of Avinguda Primavera
is the surprisingly pleasant main
tourist zone, the domineering
lines of its flashy hotels broken
by low-rise villas and landscaped
side streets. To the north are the
Salines de S'Avall, the saltpans
which once provided the
town with its principal source
of income. East from Plaça

Constitució along c/Major, and
then left (north) down c/Gabriel
Roca, is the **old harbour**, the
most diverting part of town.
Framed by an attractive, early
twentieth-century ensemble
of balconied houses, the port
makes the most of a handsome,
horseshoe-shaped bay. There's
nothing special to look at, but
it's a relaxing spot with a handful
of restaurants, fishing smacks, a
marina and a pocket-sized beach,
the **Platja Es Port**. From here,
it's a five-minute walk along
the footpath north round the
bay onto the slender, low-lying
headland that accommodates the
much more extensive sands of
the **Platja d'es Dolç**.

Es Trenc

One of Colònia de Sant Jordi's
attractions is its proximity to **Es
Trenc**, a four-kilometre strip of
sandy beach that extends as far
as the eye can see. It's neither
unknown, nor unspoilt, but the
crowds are easily absorbed except
at the height of high season,
and development is virtually
nonexistent. To drive there, head

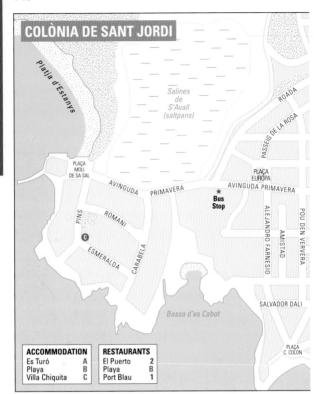

COLÒNIA DE SANT JORDI

Platja d'Estanys

Salines de S'Avall (saltpans)

ROADA

PASSEIG DE LA ROSA

PLAÇA MOLÍ DE SA SAL

AVINGUDA PRIMAVERA

PLAÇA EUROPA

AVINGUDA PRIMAVERA

Bus Stop

ALEJANDRO FARNESIO

AMISTAD

POU DEN VERVERA

PINS

ROMANI

ESMERALDA

CARRABELA

C

SALVADOR DALI

Bassa d'es Cabot

PLAÇA C. COLON

ACCOMMODATION		RESTAURANTS	
Es Turó	A	El Puerto	2
Playa	B	Playa	B
Villa Chiquita	C	Port Blau	1

north from Colònia de Sant Jordi and, about 0.5km out of town, turn left towards Campos; then, after another 2.8km, take the signed left turn and follow the country lanes leading across the saltflats to the large car park (€6) at the east end of the beach – a total distance of around 6km. This end of the beach is far more appealing than the other, at Ses Covetes, which is splotched by improvised shacks and drinks stalls.

Salines de Llevant

The saltpans backing onto Es Trenc – the **Salines de Llevant** – and the surrounding farm and scrubland support a wide variety of birdlife. Residents such as marsh harriers, kestrels, spotted crakes, fan-tailed warblers and hoopoes make a visit enjoyable at any time of year, but the best time to come is in the spring when hundreds of migrants arrive from Africa. Commonly seen in the springtime are avocets, little ringed plovers, little egrets, common sandpipers, little stints, black-tailed godwits, collared pratincoles and black terns. Several footpaths lead from Es Trenc beach into the saltpans, but it's not a good area to explore on foot: the scenery is boring, it's smelly and for

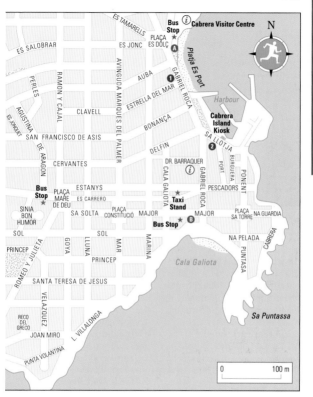

much of the year insects are a menace. It's much better to drive or cycle round using the maze-like network of narrow country lanes that traverse the saltpans, stopping anywhere that looks promising.

Cabrera island

The **Illa de Cabrera** ("Goat Island") is a bumpy, scrub- and tree-covered chunk of rock lying 18km offshore from Colònia de Sant Jordi. Boat trips depart from here, operated by Excursions Cabrera (March–Oct 1 daily; 7–8hr return including 3–4hr on the island; €35; ☎971 649034,

Ⓦwww.excursionsacabrera.com), who have an **information/ reservation office** down on the harbour. Note that there's nowhere to eat on Cabrera, so you'll either have to take your own food or shell out an extra €7 for the boat company's buffet, with drinks an added extra.

Largely bare, almost entirely uninhabited and no more than 7km wide and 5km long, Cabrera Island is nonetheless easily the largest of a cluster of tiny islets that comprise the Cabrera archipelago. The only significant hint of Cabrera's eventful past is the protective

▲ CABRERA ISLAND FERRY

castle above its supremely sheltered harbour. Pliny claimed the island to have been the birthplace of Hannibal; medieval pirates hunkered down here to plan future raids; and during the Napoleonic Wars, the Spanish stuck nine thousand French prisoners of war out on the island and promptly forgot about them – two-thirds died from hunger and disease during their four-year captivity. More recently, the island was taken over by Franco's armed forces, and now they've departed the island has been protected as the **Parc National de Cabrera**.

The day-trip starts with a sixty-minute voyage to the island. On the final stretch, the boat nudges round a hostile-looking headland to enter the harbour, **Es Port** – a narrow finger of calm water edged by hills and equipped with a tiny jetty. National Park personnel meet the boat to advise about what visitors can do and where – some parts of Cabrera are out of bounds – and there's a small park information office by the jetty too. The most popular excursion is the stiff, thirty-minute hoof up the path to the

ruins of the fourteenth-century **castle**, which perches high up on Cabrera's west coast. The views from the fortress back to Mallorca are magnificent, and all sorts of **birds** can be seen gliding round the sea-cliffs, including Manx and Cory's shearwaters and the rare Audouin's gulls, as well as peregrine falcons and shags. It is, however, the blue-underbellied **Lilfords wall lizard** that really steals the show: after you've completed the walk to the castle, take time to have a drink down by the jetty, where you can tempt the Lilfords lizards out from the scrub with pieces of fruit.

As an alternative to the castle, it's an easy fifteen-minute walk round the harbour to **Sa Plageta beach**, or you can sign up for a guided tour inland to the sombre **memorial** commemorating the dead French prisoners of war: the path to the memorial begins at Sa Plageta and takes about twenty minutes to walk, but currently you're not allowed to do it without a guide. The excursion includes a visit to a small **museum**, in a former wine cellar and grain warehouse, which traces the history of the island illustrated by a ragbag of archeological finds recovered from the island and its surrounding waters.

On the return journey, the boat bobs across the bay to visit **Sa Cova Blava** (Blue Grotto), sailing right into the cave through the fifty-metre-wide entrance and on into the yawning chamber beyond. The grotto reaches a height of 160m and is suffused by the bluish light, from which it gets its name; you can swim here too.

Llucmajor and Capocorb Vell

A middling market town, **Llucmajor** was long the centre of the island's shoemaking industry. It also has one historic claim to fame for it was here, just outside the old city walls, that Jaume III, the last of the independent kings of Mallorca, was defeated and killed by Pedro IV of Aragón – and centuries of Balearic neglect were to follow. Llucmajor is at the head of the byroad which leads south to Cap Blanc. About 13km along this road lies **Capocorb Vell** (often signposted in Castilian as "Capicorp Vey"; Mon–Wed & Fri–Sun 10am–4pm; €2), whose extensive remains date from around 1000 BC. Surrounded by arid scrubland and enclosed within a modern dry-stone wall, this prehistoric village incorporates the battered ruins of five *talayot*s and 28 dwellings. A footpath weaves round the haphazard remains, but most of what you see fails to inspire and gives little idea of how the village was arranged. The most impressive features are the Cyclopean walls, which reach a height of four metres in places. To make more sense of it all,

pick up the free English leaflet at the entrance.

Accommodation

Ermita de Nostra Senyora de Bonany

Puig Bonany, Petra ☎971 826568. Some 5km southwest of Petra (see p.134), this hilltop former monastery offers five simple double rooms. There's hot water (in one bathroom) and cooking facilities, but you'll have to bring your own food and bedding. To get there, take the Felanitx road out of Petra and look out for the sign on the edge of the village; the monastery is at the end of a bumpy, four-kilometre country lane. €15 per person.

Finca/Hotel Es Castell

c/Binibona s/n, near Inca ☎971 875154, ⊛www.fincaescastell.com. First-rate hotel in a tastefully restored old stone *finca* with an outside pool and grand views back down the valley below. It's located about 8km north of Inca amidst the foothills of the Serra de Tramuntana near the hamlet of Binibona. €125.

Hostal Ca's Bombu

c/Elionor Servera 86, Cala Rajada ☎971 563203, ⊛www.casbombu .com. This eminently appealing, family-run two-star *hostal* is kitted out in a happy version of traditional Spanish style with a pool and terrace restaurant. Breakfast included; great value at €40.

Hostal Es Turó

Plaça Es Dolç s/n, Colònia de Sant Jordi ☎971 65 50 57, ⊛www .hostalesturo.com. Unassuming, recently revamped one-star *hostal* in a solid three-storey building plonked right on Es Port beach. There's a rooftop swimming pool and eighteen guest rooms – those at the back look out over the beach. Closed Nov–April. €50.

Hostal Playa

c/Major 25, Colònia de Sant Jordi ☏971 655256, ⓦwww .restauranteplaya.com. About five minutes' walk from the main harbour, this eminently appealing little place has seven double rooms, four of which – and these are the ones you want – look out over the sea as it laps against the beach to the rear of the *hostal*. The rooms are pretty basic, but they are quite large, and each of the sea-facing rooms has a balcony. The public area is delightfully old-fashioned with oodles of wood, old photos and plates stuck on the walls. Breakfast is served on a pretty, sea-facing patio terrace, which doubles as a restaurant (see opposite). €70.

Hotel Can Moragues

Pou Nou 12, Artà ☏971 82 95 09, ⓦwww.canmoragues.com. Decorated in calming shades of yellow and cream, this hotel's eight comfortable rooms oversee a courtyard garden with a small swimming pool and sauna – the two ground-floor rooms give directly onto the garden, the others are upstairs. Opened in 1998, this four-star hotel has proved very popular. €125.

Hotel Playa Mondragó

Cala Mondragó ☏971 657752, ⓦwww.playamondrago.com. Straightforward, modern, two-star hotel with forty plain but perfectly adequate rooms in a great location – a short walk from Cala Mondragó beach. Closed Nov–March. €70.

Hotel Ses Rotges

c/Rafael Blanes 21, Cala Rajada ☏971 563108, ⓦwww.sesrotges .com. Delightful three-star establishment in an elegantly restored antique villa just out of earshot of the main square. Each of the 24 guest rooms has a beamed ceiling and a tiled floor. The hotel restaurant is the classiest in town (see p.152). Closed Nov–March. €90.

Hotel Villa Chiquita

c/Esmeralda 14, Colònia de Sant Jordi ☏971 655121, ⓦwww .hotelvillachiquita.com. This smart and well-tended hotel occupies a rambling, *pueblo*-style modern villa in the tourist zone at the west end of Avinguda Primavera. It has a good-looking garden, with lots of exotic cacti, and eighteen smartly decorated en-suite guest rooms. Closed Nov to mid-Feb. €140.

Santuari de Nostra Senyora de Cura

Puig Randa, Algaida ☏971 120260, ⓦwww.santuariodecura.com. This one-time monastery, on top of Puig Randa near Algaida, offers recently refurbished, plain but pleasant en-suite rooms in its guest quarters – a self-contained, modern block opposite the chapel. €60.

Santuari de Sant Salvador

Puig de Sant Salvador ☏971 827282. Perched on top of the 510-metre Puig de Sant Salvador, some six kilometres east of Felanitx, this former monastery holds twenty-four really rather comfortable modern guest rooms, all en suite, in a recently added wing. The monastery also has a café, but confirm its opening times if you're going to arrive hungry. €35.

Restaurants

Café Parisien

c/Ciutat 18, Artà ☏ 971 835440. Closed Sun lunch. Chic little bistro with an outside terrace and slick modern decor serving tasty *tapas* and salads at reasonable prices. C/Ciutat is Artà's short main street.

Celler Es Grop

c/Major 18, Sineu ☏ 971 520187. Closed Sun & Mon eve. Traditional bar-restaurant, whose cavernous interior doubles as a wine vault – hence the enormous wooden barrels. Serves hearty, inexpensive snacks from as little as €5; €20 for a full meal. Heaving on Wed when the town plays host to one of Mallorca's biggest fresh produce and livestock markets. Just off the town's main square, Sa Plaça.

Restaurant Ca'n Balaguer

c/Ciutat 19, Artà ☏ 971 835003. Daily 11am–10pm. Good, old-fashioned restaurant specializing in traditional Catalan dishes – and an excellent place to try salted cod, long an island favourite. Reasonable prices too.

Restaurant El Puerto

c/Port 2, Colònia de Sant Jordi ☏ 971 656047. Daily noon–4.30pm & 7–11pm. Down on the harbour, this smart and popular café-restaurant does a good trade in *tapas* and *racions* for €6–10. They also serve up a wide range of full-scale seafood dishes, including a delicious paella made from fish caught off Cabrera.

Restaurant Es Reco de Randa

c/Font 21, Randa ☏ 971 660997. Daily noon–4.30pm & 7–11pm. Randa is a pretty little hamlet of old stone houses at the foot of Puig Randa, near Algaida, (see p.130). The village holds a three-star hotel, the *Es Reco de Randa*, and this has a delightful terraced restaurant, whose specialities include roast lamb and suckling pig. Main courses average around €20.

Restaurant Flamingo

c/Bordils s/n, Porto Cristo ☏ 971 822259. Closed Nov–Feb. Informal, popular restaurant with an outdoor terrace overlooking the sea. The home-made paellas are delicious or try the steamed mussels or mixed fish grill (€20).

Restaurante Hostal Playa

c/Major 25, Colònia de Sant Jordi ☏ 971 655256. Tues–Sun noon–3.30pm & 7.30–11pm, Mon 7.30–11pm. The restaurant of the *Hostal Playa* (see opposite) may lack a few frills, but there's no complaining about the food – fish and more fish prepared in the traditional Mallorcan manner. The restaurant occupies a very pleasant, sea-facing patio-terrace. Main courses average around €20.

Restaurant La Fragua

c/Es Pla d'en Coset 3, Capdepera ☏ 971 565050. Dinner only from 7.30pm; closed Tues. The classiest restaurant in Capdepera, this intimate, romantic spot serves delicious meals from a menu featuring mainland Spanish dishes at surprisingly affordable prices. It is located just off the main square, Plaça de L'Orient, on the way up towards the castle steps.

Restaurant Port Blau

c/Gabriel Roca 67, Colònia de Sant Jordi ☏ 971 656555. Closed

PLACES

Southern Mallorca

▲ RESTAURANT SES ROTGES

Tues & Dec & Jan. This smart restaurant lives up to its smashing harbourside location with some of the town's top food, including big, beautifully presented portions of the freshest fish, plus heaped salads and great bread. Mains hover around €25.

Restaurant Ses Rotges

c/Rafael Blanes 21, Cala Rajada ☎971 563108. Closed Nov–March. The pick of Cala Rajada's many restaurants in the hotel of the same name (see p.150). Fish is the speciality here with main courses between €25–30.

Shopping

Sineu market

Sineu. Wed all day. Sineu market is the largest livestock market on the island, and the one place where you're likely to spot the rare Mallorcan black pig – either alive or in a sausage. Cheese, fruit and veg stalls also, plus tourist knick-knacks. Get there early – say 8am – to avoid the crush.

Ceramiques de Santanyí

c/Guardia Civil 22, Santanyí ☎971 163128. Mon–Fri 10am–1.30pm & 5–7.30pm, Sat 10am–1pm. Specialist producer of handmade ceramics, many with an especially pleasing metallic glaze.

Gordiola Glassworks

Ctra Palma–Manacor, Km 19 ☎971 665046. June–Sept Mon–Sat 9am–8pm, Sun 9am–1.30pm; Oct–May Mon–Sat 9am–6.30pm, Sun 9am–1.30pm; free. Gordiola has been churning out glassware for a couple of hundred years (see p.128) and today's factory has a couple of large and well-stocked gift shops. Here, you'll find everything from the most abysmal tourist tat to works of great delicacy, notably green-tinted chandeliers of traditional Mallorcan design costing anything up to €2000.

Miquel Oliver wine shop

c/Font 26, Petra ☎971 561117. Mon–Fri 9am–1pm & 2.30–6pm. The bodega of Miquel Oliver, one of the leading names of the well-regarded group of wines that carry the Pla i Llevant DO (Denominació d'Origen) name, is bang in the centre of Petra. Oliver is best known for a dry white, Muscat Original, which has garnered a cupboardful of awards.

Essentials

Arrival

The vast majority of visitors to Mallorca fly there, landing at the island's one and only international **airport**, a gleaming modern structure just 11km east of Palma, the capital. Palma is also the site of the island's main **ferry port** with services from the Spanish mainland and the other principal Balearic islands, Ibiza and Menorca. There are also ferries from Menorca to Port d'Alcúdia, on Mallorca's northern shore.

By plane

Mallorca's international airport has one enormous terminal, which handles both scheduled and charter flights, with separate floors for arrivals (downstairs) and departures (upstairs). On the arrivals floor, a flotilla of car-rental outlets jostles for position by the luggage carousels. Beyond, through the glass doors, is the main arrivals hall, which has 24-hour ATMs and currency exchange facilities, plus a provincial tourist office (Mon–Sat 9am–6pm, Sun 9am–1pm) with oodles of information, including lists of hotels and *hostals*. They will not, however, help arrange (last-minute) accommodation and neither will most of the package-tour travel agents. An exception is the extremely helpful Prima Travel (☎ 971 260143, ✆ www.prima-travel.com), which has a good selection of hotels, apartments and villas in all price ranges, plus English-speaking staff.

The least expensive way to get from the airport to Palma is by bus #1 (daily every 15min, 6am – 2.30am; €1.85), which leaves from the main entrance of the terminal building, just behind the taxi rank. These buses reach the city's inner ring road near the foot of Avinguda Gabriel Alomar i Villalonga, at the c/Joan Maragall junction, then head on to Plaça Espanya, on the north side of the centre, before continuing west to the Passeig Mallorca and then south to the top of Avinguda Jaume III. There are frequent stops along the way. A taxi from the airport to the city centre will set you back between €20 and €25.

By ferry and catamaran from mainland Spain

Three companies – Acciona Trasmediterranea, Iscomar and Balearia – operate a dense network of car ferry and catamaran services between mainland Spain and the Balearic islands. All three apply a complex fare structure that takes into account the time of year, your length of stay, your accommodation on board and any accompanying vehicle. That said, all things being equal, the cost of a car ferry or catamaran ticket is roughly the same no matter which mainland ferry port you depart from and which island you sail to. Thus, it costs about the same to get from Valencia to Palma as it does to get from Barcelona to Maó. Setting aside special deals and packages, a return ticket is about twice as much as a single. As a sample fare, the price of a passenger ticket (without a cabin) from Barcelona to Palma with Balearia costs €60–130 on a car ferry and €80–170 on a catamaran; cars cost €160 and €280 respectively. As regards sailing times, a regular car ferry takes eight hours to get from Barcelona to Palma, just over half that on a catamaran.

In all cases, advance booking is recommended and is well-nigh essential if you're taking a vehicle or need a cabin. Tickets can be purchased at the port of embarkation or in advance by phone and online. In the UK, Southern Ferries (☎ 0800/082 2010, ✆ www.southern-ferries.com) is Trasmediterranea's official agent and is good for ferry bookings with other companies too.

Palma ferry terminal is about 4km west of the city centre. Bus #1 (6am–2.30am; €1.10) leaves every fifteen minutes from

Balearic ferry and catamaran companies and routings

Acciona Trasmediterranea ☎902 45 46 45, ✆www.directferries.co.uk or ✆www.trasmediterranea.es

Barcelona to: Ciutadella, Ibiza, Maó, Palma and Port d'Alcúdia.

Denia to: Formentera, Ibiza and Palma.

Ibiza to: Barcelona, Denia, Formentera, Palma and Valencia

Maó to: Barcelona, Palma, Port d'Alcúdia, Valencia.

Palma to: Barcelona, Ibiza, Maó, and Valencia.

Port d'Alcúdia to: Barcelona, Ciutadella and Maó.

Valencia to: Ibiza, Maó and Palma.

Balearia ☎902 16 01 80, ✆www.balearia.net/eng

Barcelona to: Ciutadella, Maó, Palma and Port d'Alcúdia.

Ciutadella to: Barcelona and Port d'Alcúdia.

Denia to: Formentera, Ibiza and Palma.

Ibiza to: Denia, Formentera and Palma.

Palma to: Barcelona, Denia and Ibiza.

Port d'Alcúdia to: Barcelona and Ciutadella.

Iscomar ☎902 11 91 28, ✆www.iscomar.com

Barcelona to: Ciutadella, Ibiza, Maó, Palma and Port d'Alcúdia

Ciutadella to: Barcelona and Port d'Alcúdia.

Denia to: Formentera, Ibiza and Palma.

Palma to: Barcelona, Denia, and Valencia.

Port d'Alcúdia to: Barcelona, Ciutadella and Maó.

Valencia to: Ibiza, Maó and Palma.

outside Terminal 2 bound for the Plaça Espanya. There are also taxi ranks outside the terminal buildings; the fare to the city centre is about €10. Port d'Alcúdia is about ten minutes' walk from the resort's main harbour-marina.

Ferries and catamarans between the Balearic islands

The same three companies – Acciona Trasmediterranea, Iscomar and Balearia – also operate inter-island car ferries and catamarans. There are frequent sailings between Mallorca and Menorca and Mallorca and Ibiza, but vessels linking Menorca and Ibiza are always routed via Mallorca; Formentera, the fourth and smallest of the inhabited Balearic islands, is only linked by ferry to its neighbour, Ibiza, and the mainland port of Denia. Once again, costings are complicated, but as a sample fare, a one-way passenger ticket on a car ferry from Palma to Ibiza with Balearia costs €40 and up, from €50 on a catamaran; cars up to 6m in length cost €100 and €180 respectively; note also that car hire companies never let you take their cars from one island to another. Journey times are manageable: Ibiza to Palma is 4hr by car ferry, half that by catamaran; and Maó to Palma six hours by car ferry, three hours thirty minutes by catamaran.

Information and websites

In Mallorca, the main provincial and municipal tourist offices are in Palma (see p.54). They will provide free maps of the town and the island, plus leaflets detailing all sorts of island-wide practicalities – from bus and train timetables to lists of car rental firms, ferry schedules and boat excursion organizers. Outside Palma, many of the larger towns and resorts have seasonal tourist offices, but these vary enormously in quality, and while they are generally extremely useful for local information, they cannot be relied on to know anything about what goes on outside their patch. Opening hours vary considerably. The larger tourist offices are all open at least from Monday to Friday from 8 or 9am to 2 or 3pm. The smaller concerns operate from April or May to September or October, often on weekday mornings only.

As yet, the Internet hasn't really taken off in Mallorca. Many sites emanating from the islands are rudimentary and

Useful websites

🌐 **http://tib.caib.es** This is the official, multilingual website of tib (Transport de les Illes Baleares) and it displays all of Mallorca's train and bus timetables.

🌐 **www.palmademallorca.es** The official website of Palma, multilingual and with a battery of information, including "where to go" and "what's on" sections.

🌐 **www.baleares.com/tourist.guide/cycling** Details of eight different cycle routes on Mallorca, from 70km to 320km. Routes are designed to avoid busy roads and to provide sections on the flat as well as steep climbs. In several languages, including English.

🌐 **www.inm.es** Daily weather forecasts for the whole of Spain – in Spanish.

🌐 **www.majorcadailybulletin.es** Online edition of Mallorca's leading English-language newspaper.

🌐 **www.mallorca-restaurants-121.com** There are lots of websites recommending island restaurants, but this is the pick.

🌐 **www.mallorcaweb.com** Compendious website dedicated to the island, covering everything from art culture through to restaurants, politics and economics.

🌐 **www.okspain.org** Official site of the US's SNTO.

🌐 **www.spain.info** Official website of the Spanish National Tourist Office (SNTO). Provides an excellent general introduction to the country as a whole, and its myriad synopses – on everything from national parks to accommodation – are concise and clearly, even temptingly written.

🌐 **www.tourspain.co.uk** Official site of the UK's SNTO.

🌐 **www.illesbalears.es** The Balearic government's official English-language tourist site with separate sections for all of the islands. Covers a wide range of topics – from shopping through to nature – but many of the synopses are more than a little terse. Clearly laid out; a useful introduction.

🌐 **www.winesfromspain.com** Smashing introduction to the wines of Spain with precise definitions of all the various Denominaciones d'Origen (DOs), including Mallorca's two DOs, Pla i Llevant and Binissalem.

infrequently updated, and the majority are only available in Castilian (Spanish) or Catalan, though you can get help in deciphering these from any Internet translation service. The main exception is the island's hotels, for whom having a website is becoming pretty much de rigueur.

Maps

Detailed road maps of Mallorca are widely available from island newsagents, petrol stations, souvenir shops and bookshops. There are several different types on offer and prices vary considerably, but you shouldn't have to pay more than €5. If you do buy a map, it's important to get a Catalan version: all island road, town and street signs are in Catalan, but many of the maps on sale are in Castilian (Spanish) and are, therefore, impossibly confusing to use. To ensure you're buying a Catalan map, check out the spelling of Port de Pollença on Mallorca's north coast; if it reads "Puerto de Pollença", you've got a Castilian version.

Currently, the most up-to-date road maps are produced by Triangle Postals (Ⓦ www.trianglepostals.com), who publish *Mallorca* (1:130,000) This map accurately portray the island's highways and principal byways along with topographical details, but doesn't have an index; it is hard to find on the island itself – best to get a copy before you go. The *Rough Guide Map to Mallorca* (1:80,000) is equally difficult to locate on the islands, but it does have an index and although the road numbers are the old ones, it is more detailed than all of its main rivals. More readily available in the Balearics is GeoCenter's clear and easy-to-use *Leisure Map Mallorca* (1:120,000) and the *Berlitz Holiday Map Menorca* (1:55000).

Both of these usefully indicate distances between settlements and mark salient geographical features, but neither has an index and both have the old road numbers. The best town and resort maps are produced by Distrimapas Telstar (Ⓦ www .distrimapas-telstar.es) at the 1:10,000 to 1:15,000 scales; they cost about €5–7 each and are widely available.

Of the several Mallorca hiking maps on the market, the classiest are those published by a German company, Reise Know-How (Ⓦ www.reise-know-how.de), whose products are available direct from the company or internationally at leading bookstores at about £9/€15 – but not in the Balearics themselves. It publishes four large, topographical maps of Mallorca (1:40,000) – North, East, South and West – each of which is marked with all the main hiking trails and bicycle routes. Their only serious competitor is Editorial Alpina (Ⓦ www.editorialalpina. com), a Spanish company which publishes three multilingual *Map & Hiking Guides* to the Tramuntana mountains – one each for the North, Centre and South. The guide books give the lowdown on a variety of hikes in reasonable detail and the maps (at 1:25,000) are the most detailed on the market. Each map and guide costs €9 each and is widely available across Mallorca – at, for example, Sóller tourist office.

Transport

Mallorca has a reliable bus network between all of its major settlements, a multitude of taxis, a plethora of car-rental firms and plenty of bicycles and mopeds to hire, as well as a couple of very useful train lines.

Buses

Palma is the hub of the island's extensive bus network and from here it's possible to reach most of the villages and resorts of the coast and interior with ease. These main routes are supplemented by more intermittent local services between the smaller towns of the interior and between neighbouring resorts.

Buses in Palma and the adjacent Bay of Palma resorts are all operated by EMT (Empresa Municipal de Transports; see box below); the rest of the island is served by a bewildering range of bus companies, though their services are co-ordinated by tib (Transports de les Illes Balears; see box below). There is an excellent tib bus information centre at the main bus station in Palma, a few minutes' walk from the Plaça Espanya.

As for ticket prices, distances are small – it is, for example, only 110km from Andratx in the west to Cala Rajada in the east – and consequently travel costs are low: the one-way fare from Palma to Port de Sóller, for instance, is just €2.50.

Passengers buy tickets from the driver, unless they've been bought in advance at a bus station. For the most part, bus stops are clearly indicated with brightly coloured signs, but in some of the country towns and villages they can be very hard to find. Remember also that bus services are drastically reduced on Sundays and holidays, and it's best not even to consider travelling out into the sticks on these days. The Catalan words to look out for on timetables are *diari* (daily), *feiners* (workdays, including Saturday), *diumenge* (Sunday) and *festius* (holidays). Local bus timetables are available at most tourist offices.

Trains

Mallorca has its own train network. One line travels through the mountains from Palma to Sóller (28km), the second shuttles across the flatlands of the interior from Palma to Binissalem and then Inca, just beyond which it forks, with one branch nudging south to Sineu, Petra and Manacor, the other pushing on to Sa Pobla. Work is under way to extend the line from Sa Pobla to Alcúdia. Each line has its own station in Palma near Plaça Espanya. The trip to Sóller takes about an hour and passes through some of the island's most magnificent scenery. The Inca line is much less scenically enjoyable, but the service is much more frequent with three or four departures hourly. It takes forty minutes to get from Palma to Inca, twenty minutes more to Sa Pobla. The standard return fare from Palma to Inca is just €5.

Car rental

Car-rental companies throng the island's resorts, larger towns and airport. All the major international players have outlets,

---

Bus and train information

For bus timetable information in Palma and the Bay of Palma, call EMT on ☎971 214444 or visit ⊛www.emtpalma.es. Outside of Palma and its environs, call tib ☎971 177777 (Spanish and Catalan only).

The Palma–Sóller train has its own information line and website, ☎ 971 752051, ⊛www.trendesoller.com. For timetable information on the Palma–Inca–Sa Pobla/ Manacor line, call ☎971 177777 (again, Spanish and Catalan only).

and there are dozens of small, local companies too. To rent a car, you'll have to be 21 or over (and have been driving for at least a year), and you'll probably need a credit card – though some places will accept a hefty deposit in cash and some smaller companies simply ignore all the normal regulations.

Cycling

Cycling can be an inexpensive and flexible way of getting around Mallorca, though you have to be pretty fit to tackle the steep hills of the northern part of the island. The Spanish are keen cycling fans, which means that you'll (usually) find reasonable facilities and respectful car drivers.

Renting a bike costs anywhere between about €5 and €8 a day for an ordinary bike (€27 to €40 per week), or about thirty percent more for a mountain bike. Renting is straightforward: there are dozens of suppliers (there's usually one at every resort) and tourist offices can provide a list or advise you of the nearest outlet.

Accommodation

Package-tour operators have a stranglehold on thousands of Mallorcan hotel rooms, villas and apartments, but nevertheless reasonably priced rooms are still available to the independent traveller even if options can be limited at the height of the season, when advance reservations are strongly recommended. Most hoteliers speak at least a modicum of English, so visitors who don't speak Catalan or Spanish can usually book over the phone, but a confirmation letter or email is always a good idea. In Mallorca the easiest place to get a room on spec is Palma, with Sóller and Port de Sóller lagging not far behind, and there are usually vacancies at the five island monasteries that offer frugal accommodation in remote hilltop locations.

Types of accommodation

It's often worth bargaining over hotel room prices outside the peak season, since the posted tariff doesn't necessarily mean much. Many hotels have rooms at different prices, and tend to offer the more expensive ones first. Most places also have rooms with three or four beds at not a great deal more than the price of a double room, which represents a real saving for families and small groups. On the other hand, people travelling alone invariably end up paying over the odds.

Incidentally, many establishments are signed as *hostals*, though there is little difference between a *hostal* and a hotel.

Fincas

Many of Mallorca's old stone *fincas* (farmhouses) have been snaffled up for use as second homes, and many are now leased by their owners to package-tour operators for the whole or part of the season. Out of the tour operators' main season, these *fincas* often stand idle. At any time of the year, though preferably well in advance of your holiday, it's worth approaching the Associació Agroturisme Balear, Avgda Gabriel Alomar i Villalonga 8a–2a, 07006 Palma (☎ 971 721508, ⓦ www.agroturismo-balear.com), which issues a booklet detailing most of the finest *fincas* and takes bookings. Although some *fincas* are modest affairs and still a part of working farms, the majority are comparatively luxurious and many are situated in remote and beautiful spots. They are not, however, cheap: prices range from €40 to €80 per person per night, and a minimum length of stay of anything between two nights and one week is often stipulated.

Sports and activities

During the day at least, tourist life on Mallorca is centred on the beach. There are long and generous strands at several of the major resorts – such as Port d'Alcúdia, S'Arenal and Port de Pollença – and several dozen much smaller cove **beaches**, like the ones at Deià and Estellencs. At all the larger resorts, an army of companies offers equipment hire for a wide range of beach sports and activities, from **sailing** and pedalo pedalling through to jet-skiing and **windsurfing**. There are sandcastle-building competitions too, as well as some scuba-diving, though the underwater world off Mallorca lacks colour and clarity – the best **diving** is around the islet of Sa Dragonera on the

west coast and off Cala Figuera on the east coast. If you're keen to participate in any of these activities, there's no need to make advance reservations – just turn up early(ish) in the morning and off you go.

Away from the coast, **cycling** is a popular pastime as are **horse and pony riding** – indeed, Mallorca is dotted with stables and crisscrossed by bridle paths. Even more popular, however, is **hiking**, with hundreds of hikers descending on the Serra de Tramuntana mountains in the spring and autumn, necessarily out of the heat of the summer sun. It is also encouraging to note that the island's hiking trails, which were once notorious for their poor signage, are in the process of being re-signed.

Useful contacts for sport and activities

Hiking: Headwater (UK ☎01606/720033, ☻www.headwater.com) is a well-regarded walking-tour specialist providing guided hikes in the Serra de Tramuntana mountains. Its standard eight-day guided hike takes place from mid-September to November and from February to April.

Horse riding: A full list of Mallorcan horse-riding companies is provided on ☻www .mallorcaonline.com/sport/equitau.htm.

Sailing and Windsurfing: Sail & Surf Pollença (☎971 865346, ☻www.sailsurf.de). Well-regarded, German-run specialists in sailing and windsurfing.

Festivals

January

16: Revetla de Sant Antoni Abat (Eve of St Antony Abbot's Day) is celebrated by the lighting of bonfires (*foguerons*) in Palma and several of Mallorca's villages, especially Sa Pobla and Muro. In the latter, the villagers move from fire to fire, dancing round in fancy dress and eating *espinagades*, traditional eel and vegetable patties.

17: Beneides de Sant Antoni (Blessing of St Antony). St Antony's feast day is marked by processions in many of

Mallorca's country towns, notably Sa Pobla and Artà, with farmyard animals herded through the streets to receive the saint's blessing and protection against disease.

19: Revetla de Sant Sebastià Palma has more bonfires, singing and dancing for St Sebastian.

20: Festa de Sant Sebastià Pollença procession led by a holy banner (*estenard*) picturing the saint. It's accompanied by *cavallets* (literally "merry-go-rounds"), two young dancers each wearing a cardboard horse and imitating the animal's walk. You'll see *cavallets*, which are of medieval origin, at many of the island's festivals.

February

Carnaval Lots of towns and villages live it up during the week before Lent with marches and fancy dress parades. The biggest and liveliest is in Palma, where the shindig is known as *Sa Rua* (the Cavalcade).

March/April

Setmana Santa (Holy Week) is as keenly observed in Mallorca as it is everywhere else in Spain. On Maundy Thursday in Palma, a much-venerated icon of the crucified Christ, *La Sang*, is taken from the eponymous church on the Plaça del Hospital (off La Rambla) and paraded through the city streets. There are also solemn Good Friday (*Divendres Sant*) processions in many towns and villages, with the more important taking place in Palma and Sineu. Most holy of all, however, is the Good Friday *Davallament* (The Lowering), the culmination of Holy Week in Pollença. Here, in total silence and by torchlight, the inhabitants lower a figure of Christ down from the hilltop *oratori* to the church of Nostra Senyora dels Àngels. During Holy Week there are also many *romerias* (pilgrimages) to the island's holy places, with one of the most popular being the climb up to the Ermita Santa Magdalena, near Inca. The Monestir de Lluc, which possesses Mallorca's most venerated shrine, is another religious focus during

this time, with the penitential trudging round its Camí dels Misteris del Rosari (Way of the Mysteries of the Rosary).

May

Mid-May: Sa Firá i Es Firó in Port de Sóller features mock battles between Christians and infidels in commemoration of the thrashing of a band of Arab pirates in 1561. Lots of booze and firing of antique rifles into the air.

June

Early to mid-June: Corpus Christi At noon in the main square of Pollença an ancient and curious dance of uncertain provenance takes place – the *Ball de les Àguiles* (Dance of the Eagles) – followed by a religious procession.

July

Last Sunday: Festa de Sant Jaume This festival in Alcúdia celebrates the feast day of St James with a popular religious procession followed by folk dances, fireworks and the like.

August

2: Mare de Déu dels Àngels Moors and Christians battle it out again, this time in Pollença.
20: Cavallet (see 20 January above) dances in Felanitx.

September

Second week: Nativitat de Nostra Senyora (Nativity of the Virgin). In Alaró,

Public holidays

January 1 New Year's Day (Cap d'Any)
January 6 Epiphany (Reyes Magos)
Maundy Thursday (Dijous Sant)
Good Friday (Divendres Sant)
May 1 Labour Day (Día del Treball)
August 15 Assumption of the Virgin (Assumpció)
October 12 Spanish National Day (Día de la Hispanidad)
November 1 All Saints (Tots Sants)
December 6 Constitution Day (Día de la Constitució)
December 8 Immaculate Conception (Inmaculada Concepción)
December 24 Christmas Eve
December 25 Christmas Day (Nadal; Navidad in Castilian)
December 26 Boxing Day/St Stephen's Day (Dia de Sant Esteban)

honouring the Virgin with a pilgrimage to a hilltop shrine near the Castell d'Alaró.

December

Christmas (*Nadal*) is especially pictur-esque in Palma, where there are Nativity plays in the days leading up to the 25th.

Directory

Addresses These are usually abbreviated to a standard format – "c/Bellver 7" translates as Bellver Street (carrer) no. 7. Plaça means square. "Plaça Rosari 5, 2è" means on the second floor at no. 5. "Passeig d'es Born 15, 1–C" means suite C, first floor, at no. 15. "s/n" (sense número) indicates a building without a street number. In Franco's day, most avenues and boulevards were named after Fascist heroes and, although the vast majority were rechristened years ago, there's still some confusion in remoter spots. Another source of bafflement can be house numbers: some houses carry more than one number (the by-product of half-hearted reorganizations), and on many streets the sequence is impossible to fathom.

Children Most hotels, pensions and hostals welcome children and many offer rooms with three or four beds. Restaurants and cafés almost always encourage families too. Many package holidays have child-minding facilities as part of the deal. Disposable nappies and other basic supplies are widely available in the resort areas and the larger towns.

Disabilities, travellers with Despite its popularity as a holiday destination, Mallorca pays scant regard to its disabled visitors, with facilities lagging way behind those of many EU countries. That said, things are slowly improving. Hotels with wheelchair access and other appropriate facilities are increasingly common and, by law, all new public buildings in Spain are required to be fully accessible. Transport is particularly problematic, as buses are not equipped for wheelchairs, and few of the islands' car-rental firms have vehicles with adaptations – though at least the taxi drivers are usually helpful.

Doctors and dentists can be found In the resort areas and in Palma most hotel receptions will be able to find an English-speaking doctor or dentist. For complete lists look under metges (Castilian *médicos*)

or *clíniques dentals* (*clínicas dentales*) in the *Yellow Pages*.

Electricity The current is 220 volts AC, with standard European-style two-pin plugs. Brits will need an adaptor to connect their appliances, North Americans both an adaptor and a 220-to-110 transformer.

Emergencies For medical, fire and police emergencies, call ☏112.

Entry requirements Citizens of all EU and EEA countries only need a valid passport or national identity card to enter Spain, where – with some limitations – they also have the right to work, live and study. US, Australian, Canadian and New Zealand citizens need only a valid passport for visits of up to ninety days, but are not allowed to work. Non-EU citizens who wish to visit Spain for longer than ninety days must get a special visa from a Spanish consulate or embassy before departure. In all cases, your passport must be valid for the entire period of the proposed visit. Visa requirements do change and it is always advisable to check the current situation before leaving home.

Internet Most of Mallorca's better hotels provide free Internet access for their guests.

Mail The Mallorcan postal system is competent and comprehensive, with post offices (*correus*) located in every town and most larger villages. Opening hours are usually Monday to Friday 9am to 2pm, though the main post office in Palma is open through the afternoon and on Saturday mornings too. All post offices close on public holidays.

Mobile phones Mobile phone access is routine in all the larger towns and villages and in most of the countryside. Mallorca's mobile network works on GSM 900/1800, which means that mobiles bought in North America need to be triband to gain cellular access.

Money Spanish currency is the euro (€). Each euro is made up of 100 cents. Notes come in denominations of 5, 10, 50 and

Fly Less – Stay Longer!

Rough Guides believes in the good that travel does, but we are deeply aware of the impact of fuel emissions on climate change. We recommend taking fewer trips and staying for longer. If you can avoid travelling by air, please use an alternative, especially for journeys of under 1000km/600miles. And always offset your travel at ⓦ www.roughguides.com/climatechange.

500 euros, coins as 1, 2, 5, 10, 20 and 50 cents, and 1 and 2 euros. The exchange rate for the euro at time of writing was €0.67 to the British pound; €1.36 to the US dollar; €9.76 to the South African Rand; €1.44 to the Canadian dollar; €1.67 to the Australian dollar; and €1.94 to the NZ dollar. ATMs are commonplace, especially in the cities and larger resorts, and are undoubtedly the quickest and easiest way of getting money. Most ATMs give instructions in a variety of languages, and accept a host of debit cards, including all those carrying the Cirrus coding. Credit cards can be used in ATMs too, but in this case transactions are treated as loans, with interest accruing daily from the date of withdrawal. All major credit cards, including American Express, Visa and MasterCard, are widely accepted in Mallorca.

Opening hours Although there's been some movement towards a northern European working day – especially in Palma and the major tourist resorts – most shops and offices still close for a siesta of at least two hours in the hottest part of the afternoon between 1/2pm and 4/5pm. Cafés and *tapas* bars open from around 9am until at least early in the evening, and many remain open till late at night. Restaurants open from around noon until sometime between 2pm and 4pm, before reopening

in the evening from around 7/8pm until 10/11pm. Those restaurants with their eye on the tourist trade often stay open all day and can be relied upon on Sundays, when many local spots close.

Telephones You can make domestic and international telephone calls with equal ease from Spanish public (and private) phones. Most hotel rooms also have phones, but note that there is almost always an exorbitant surcharge for their use. For operator services call ☎1009. International directory enquiries are on ☎11886, within Spain ☎11888. To call Mallorca from abroad, dial your international access code, followed by ☎34 for Spain and then the nine-digit local number. Note that most Balearic phone numbers begin with ☎971, but this is an integral part of the number, not an area code.

Time Spain (and therefore Mallorca) is one hour ahead of Greenwich Mean Time, six hours ahead of US Eastern Standard Time, nine hours ahead of US Pacific Standard Time, nine hours behind Australian Eastern Standard Time and eleven hours behind New Zealand – except for periods during the changeovers made in the respective countries to and from daylight saving. In Spain, the clocks go forward an hour on the last Sunday of March and back an hour on the last Sunday of October.

Chronology

Chronology

By 4000 BC ▶ Neolithic pastoralists have established themselves on Mallorca.

1500 BC ▶ The bronze-working Beaker People supplant the pastoralists.

1500 BC–123 BC ▶ The Talayotic period. Takes its name from the *talayot*, a cone-shaped tower with a circular base, whose remains still dot the island. Construction of the island's first walled villages.

123 BC ▶ The Romans occupy Mallorca, bringing the island under their centre. The Romans introduce viticulture, and initiate olive-oil production from newly planted groves.

425 AD ▶ The Vandals sweep right across the Balearics, thereby ending Roman rule.

707–8 ▶ The Moors of North Africa mount an extended raid against Mallorca, destroying its fleet and carrying away slaves and booty.

716 ▶ The Moors complete the conquest of mainland Spain.

Early ninth century ▶ The Moors occupy Mallorca.

1162 ▶ Alfonso II unites the kingdoms of Aragón and Catalunya as Moorish power begins to wane.

1229 ▶ King Jaume I of Aragón and Catalunya captures Mallorca from the Moors.

1276 ▶ Death of King Jaume I; Jaume II becomes king of an independent Mallorca and Menorca.

1311 ▶ Death of King Jaume II; accession of his son Sancho.

1349 ▶ Pedro IV of Aragón invades Mallorca and incorporates the island within his kingdom. The unification of the Balearics with Aragón proves to be an economic disaster for the islanders.

1479 ▶ Fernando V of Aragón marries Isabella I of Castile, thereby uniting the two largest Christian kingdoms in Spain.

Sixteenth to mid-nineteenth century ▶ As trade moves west to take advantage of the conquest of South America, Mallorca becomes a neglected and impoverished backwater, subject to droughts, famines and epidemics of cholera, bubonic plague and yellow fever.

Late nineteenth century ▶ Agriculture, particularly almond cultivation, revives, though Spain as a whole is on the political and economic skids. As on the mainland, Balearic politics become polarized between conservative and liberal groupings, a chronic instability that is to be the harbinger of the military coup that ushered in a right-wing dictatorship in Madrid in 1923.

1932–36 ▶ Parliamentary government resumes, but the country remains bitterly divided between right and left.

1936–39 ▶ The Spanish Civil War. General Francisco Franco leads a successful right-wing military rebellion against the government.

Franco becomes head of state and bloody reprisals follow. Pope Pius XII congratulates the dictator on his "Catholic victory". Mallorca serves as an important base for the Fascists throughout the war.

1939–75 ▶ Franco establishes a one-party state, backed up by stringent censorship and a vigorous secret police. By staying neutral during World War II, he survives the fall of Nazi Germany. In 1969, Franco nominates the grandson of Alfonso XIII, Juan Carlos, as his successor, but retains his vice-like grip on the country until his death in 1975.

1960s ▶ Mallorca booms as a tourist destination.

1976–82 ▶ Juan Carlos recognizes the need for political reform and helps steer the country towards a parliamentary system.

1978 ▶ The Spanish parliament, the Cortes, passes a new constitution, which reorganizes the country on a more federal basis and allows for the establishment of regional Autonomous Communities.

1982–96 ▶ In 1982, Felipe González's Socialist Workers' Party – the PSOE – is elected to office. Spain's economy grows dramatically, the country becomes a respected member of the EU, and the PSOE attempts to deal with Spain's deep-seated separatist tendencies by permitting a large degree of regional autonomy.

1983 ▶ The Balearics is constituted as an autonomous region within Spain, the Comunidad Autónoma de las Islas Baleares.

1996–2003 ▶ The Conservative Popular Party wins power in Madrid, but needs the parliamentary support of Catalan nationalist deputies to govern effectively. The price is more powers to the regions.

2002 ▶ Spain enters the single-currency euro zone.

2004 ▶ The PSOE regain power in the national elections of 2004. The new administration – like its predecessors – struggles to deal with the demands of the Basque and Catalan regionalists, both of whom are determined to further distance themselves from Spain as a whole.

Language

Language

Although Catalan is the preferred/native language of most islanders, you'll almost always get by perfectly well if you speak Castilian (Spanish), as long as you're aware of the use of Catalan in timetables and so forth. Once you get into it, Castilian is one of the easiest languages there is, the rules of pronunciation pretty straightforward and strictly observed. You'll find some basic pronunciation rules for both Catalan and Castilian below, plus a selection of words and phrases in both languages. Castilian is certainly easier to pronounce, but don't be afraid to try Catalan, especially in the more out-of-the-way places – you'll generally get a good reception if you at least try communicating in the local language.

On paper, Catalan looks like a cross between French and Spanish and is generally easy to understand if you know those two, although when spoken it has a very harsh sound and is harder to get to grips with.

Numerous Spanish phrasebooks and dictionaries are available with the most user-friendly being *Rough Guide's Spanish Dictionary Phrasebook*. No English–Catalan phrasebook is currently in print and there's only one dictionary, published by Routledge.

Castilian (Spanish): a few rules

Unless there's an accent, words ending in d, l, r, and z are **stressed** on the last syllable, all others on the second to last. All **vowels** are pure and short; combinations have predictable results.

A somewhere between back and father.
E as in get.
I as in police.
O as in hot.
U as in rule.

C is lisped before E and I, hard otherwise: *cerca* is pronounced "thairka".
CH is pronounced as in English.
G is a guttural H sound (like the *ch* in

Catalan

Català is spoken by over six million people in the Balearics, Catalunya, part of Aragón, most of Valencia, Andorra and parts of the French Pyrenees; it is thus much more widely spoken than several better-known languages such as Danish, Finnish and Norwegian. It is a Romance language, stemming from Latin and more directly from medieval Provençal. Spaniards in the rest of the country often belittle it by saying that to get a *Català* word you just cut a Castilian one in half (which is often true), but in fact the grammar is much more complicated than Castilian and there are eight vowel sounds, three more than in Castilian.

loch) before E or I, a hard G elsewhere: *gigante* is pronounced "higante".

H is always silent.

J is the same sound as a guttural G: *jamón* is pronounced "hamon".

LL sounds like an English Y: *tortilla* is pronounced "torteeya".

N as in English, unless it has a tilde (ñ) over it, when it becomes NY: *mañana* sounds like "man-yaana".

QU is pronounced like an English K.

R is rolled, RR doubly so.

V sounds more like B, *vino* becoming "beano".

X has an S sound before consonants, a KS sound before vowels.

Z is the same as a soft C, so *cerveza* is pronounced "thairvaitha".

Catalan: a few rules

With *Català*, don't be tempted to use the few rules of Castilian pronunciation you may know – in particular the soft Spanish Z and C don't apply, so unlike in the rest of Spain it's not "Barthelona" but "Barcelona", as in English.

A as in hat if stressed, as in alone when unstressed.

E varies, but usually as in get.

I as in police.

IG sounds like the "tch" in the English scratch; *lleig* (ugly) is pronounced "yeah-tch".

O varies, but usually as in hot.

U lies somewhere between put and rule.

Ç sounds like an English S: *plaça* is pronounced "plassa".

C followed by an E or I is soft; otherwise hard.

G followed by E or I is like the "zh" in Zhivago; otherwise hard.

H is always silent.

J as in the French "Jean".

LL sounds like an English Y or LY, like the "yuh" sound in "million".

N as in English, though before F or V it sometimes sounds like an M.

NY replaces the Castilian Ñ.

QU before E or I sounds like K; before A or O as in "quit".

R is rolled, but only at the start of a word; at the end it's often silent.

T is pronounced as in English, though sometimes it sounds like a D, as in *viatge* or *dotze*.

TX is like the English CH.

V at the start of a word sounds like B; in all other positions it's a soft F sound.

W is pronounced like a B/V.

X is like SH in most words, though in some, like *exit*, it sounds like an X.

Z is like the English Z.

Useful words and phrases

Basics		
ENGLISH	CASTILIAN	CATALAN
Yes, No, OK	**Sí, No, Vale**	Sí, No, Val
Please, Thank you	**Por favor, Gracias**	Per favor, Gràcies
Where, When	**Dónde, Cuándo**	On, Quan
What, How much	**Qué, Cuánto**	Què, Quant
Here, There	**Aquí, Allí, Allá**	Aquí, Allí, Allà
This, That	**Esto, Eso**	Això, Allò
Now, Later	**Ahora, Más tarde**	Ara, Més tard

Open, Closed	**Abierto/a, Cerrado/a**	Obert, Tancat
With, Without	**Con, Sin**	Amb, Sense
Good, Bad	**Buen(o)/a, Mal(o)/a**	Bo(na), Dolent(a)
Big, Small	**Gran(de), Pequeño/a**	Gran, Petit(a)
Cheap, Expensive	**Barato/a, Caro/a**	Barat(a), Car(a)
Hot, Cold	**Caliente, Frío/a**	Calent(a), Fred(a)
More, Less	**Más, Menos**	Més, Menys
Today, Tomorrow	**Hoy, Mañana**	Avui, Demà
Yesterday	**Ayer**	Ahir
Day before yesterday	**Anteayer**	Abans-d'ahir
Next week	**La semana que viene**	La setmana que ve
Next month	**El mes que viene**	El mes que ve

Greetings and responses

ENGLISH	CASTILIAN	CATALAN
Hello, Goodbye	**Hola, Adiós**	Hola, Adéu
Good morning	**Buenos días**	Bon dia
Good afternoon/night	**Buenas tardes/noches**	Bona tarda/nit
See you later	**Hasta luego**	Fins després
Sorry	**Lo siento/discúlpeme**	Ho sento
Excuse me	**Con permiso/perdón**	Perdoni
How are you?	**¿Cómo está (usted)?**	Com va?
I (don't) understand	**(No) Entiendo**	(No) Ho entenc
Not at all/You're welcome	**De nada**	De res
Do you speak English?	**¿Habla (usted) inglés?**	Parla anglès?
I (don't) speak	**(No) Hablo Español**	(No) Parlo Català
My name is...	**Me llamo...**	Em dic . . .
What's your name?	**¿Cómo se llama usted?**	Com es diu?
I am English	**Soy inglés/esa**	Sóc anglès/esa
Scottish	**escocés/esa**	escocès/esa
Australian	**australiano/a**	australià/ana
Canadian	**canadiense/a**	canadenc(a)
American	**americano/a**	americà/ana
Irish	**irlandés/esa**	irlandès/esa
Welsh	**galés/esa**	gallès/esa

Hotels and transport

ENGLISH	CASTILIAN	CATALAN
I want	**Quiero**	Vull (pronounced "fwee")
I'd like	**Quisiera**	Voldria
Do you know...?	**¿Sabe...?**	Vostès saben...?
I don't know	**No sé**	No sé
There is (is there?)	**(¿)Hay(?)**	Hi ha(?)
Give me...	**Deme...**	Doneu-me...
Do you have...?	**¿Tiene...?**	Té...?
...the time	**...la hora**	...l'hora
...a room	**...una habitación**	...alguna habitació
...with two beds/	**...con dos camas/**	...amb dos llits/
double bed	**cama matrimonial**	llit per dues persones
...with shower/bath	**...con ducha/baño**	...amb dutxa/bany
for one person	**para una persona**	per a una persona
(two people)	**(dos personas)**	(dues persones)
for one night	**para una noche**	per una nit

English	CASTILIAN	CATALAN
(one week)	(una semana)	(una setmana)
It's fine, how much is it?	Está bien, ¿cuánto es?	Esta bé, quant és?
It's too expensive	Es demasiado caro	És massa car
Don't you have anything cheaper?	¿No tiene algo más barato?	En té de més bon preu?
Can one...?	¿Se puede...?	Es pot...?
...camp (near) here?	¿...acampar aquí (cerca)?	...acampar a la vora?
Is there a hostel nearby?	¿Hay un hostal aquí cerca?	Hi ha un hostal a la vora?
It's not very far	No es muy lejos	No és gaire lluny
How do I get to...?	¿Por dónde se va a...?	Per anar a...?
Left, right, straight on	Izquierda, derecha, todo recto	A l'esquerra, a la dreta, tot recte
Where is...?	¿Dónde está...?	On és...?
...the bus station	...la estación de autobuses	...l'estació de autobuses
...the bus stop	...la parada	...la parada
...the railway station	...la estación de ferrocarril	...l'estació
...the nearest bank	...el banco más cercano	...el banc més a prop
...the post office	...el correo/la oficina de correos	...l'oficina de correus
...the toilet	...el baño/aseo/servicio	...la toaleta
Where does the bus to... leave from?	¿De dónde sale el autobús... para?	De on surt el auto... bús a
Is this the train for Sóller	¿Es este el tren para Sóller?	Aquest tren va a Sóller?
I'd like a (return) ticket to...	Quisiera un billete (de ida y vuelta) para...	Voldria un bitllet (d'anar i tornar) a...
What time does it leave? (arrive in...)?	¿A qué hora sale? (llega a...)?	A quina hora surt? (arriba a...)?
What is there to eat?	¿Qué hay para comer?	Què hi ha per menjar?
What's that?	¿Qué es eso?	Què és això?

Days of the week

ENGLISH	CASTILIAN	CATALAN
Monday	lunes	dilluns
Tuesday	martes	dimarts
Wednesday	miércoles	dimecres
Thursday	jueves	dijous
Friday	viernes	divendres
Saturday	sábado	dissabte
Sunday	domingo	diumenge

Numbers

	CASTILIAN	CATALAN
1	un/uno/una	un(a)
2	dos	dos (dues)
3	tres	tres
4	cuatro	quatre
5	cinco	cinc
6	seis	sis

7	**siete**	set
8	**ocho**	vuit
9	**nueve**	nou
10	**diez**	deu
11	**once**	onze
12	**doce**	dotze
13	**trece**	tretze
14	**catorce**	catorze
15	**quince**	quinze
16	**dieciséis**	setze
17	**diecisiete**	disset
18	**dieciocho**	divuit
19	**diecinueve**	dinou
20	**veinte**	vint
21	**veintiuno**	vint-i-un
30	**treinta**	trenta
40	**cuarenta**	quaranta
50	**cincuenta**	cinquanta
60	**sesenta**	seixanta
70	**setenta**	setanta
80	**ochenta**	vuitanta
90	**noventa**	novanta
100	**cien(to)**	cent
101	**ciento uno**	cent un
102	**ciento dos**	cent dos (dues)
200	**doscientos**	dos-cents (dues-centes)
500	**quinientos**	cinc-cents
1000	**mil**	mil
2000	**dos mil**	dos mil

Food and drink

Although we've provided a reasonably extensive **Castilian and Catalan food and drink glossary** below, most restaurants, cafés and bars have **multilingual menus**, with English, Catalan and Castilian almost always three of the options. The main exceptions are out in the countryside, where there may only be a Catalan menu or maybe no menu at all, in which case the waiter will rattle off the day's dishes in Catalan or sometimes Castilian.

Basics

ENGLISH	**CASTILIAN**	CATALAN
Bread	**Pan**	Pa
Butter	**Mantequilla**	Mantega
Cheese	**Queso**	Formatge
Eggs	**Huevos**	Ous
Oil	**Aceite**	Oli
Pepper	**Pimienta**	Pebre
Salt	**Sal**	Sal
Sugar	**Azúcar**	Sucre
Vinegar	**Vinagre**	Vinagre
Garlic	**Ajo**	All
Rice	**Arroz**	Arròs

LANGUAGE

Food and drink

English	Castilian	Catalan
Fruit	**Fruta**	Fruita
Vegetables	**Verduras/Legumbres**	Verdures/Llegumos
To have breakfast	**Desayunar**	Esmorzar
To have lunch	**Almorzar**	Dinar
To have dinner	**Cenar**	Sopar
Menu	**Carta**	Menú
Bottle	**Botella**	Ampolla
Glass	**Vaso**	Got
Fork	**Tenedor**	Forquilla
Knife	**Cuchillo**	Ganivet
Spoon	**Cuchara**	Cullera
Table	**Mesa**	Taula
The bill/check	**El compte**	La cuenta
Grilled	**A la brasa**	A la planxa
Fried	**Frit**	Fregit
Stuffed/rolled	**Relleno**	Farcit
Casserole	**Guisado**	Guisat
Roast	**Asado**	Rostit

Fruit (fruita) and vegetables (verdures/llegumes)

ENGLISH	CASTILIAN	CATALAN
Apple	**Manzana**	Poma
Asparagus	**Espárragos**	Espàrrecs
Aubergine/eggplant	**Berenjenas**	Albergínies
Banana	**Plátano**	Plàtan
Carrots	**Zanahorias**	Pastanagues
Cucumber	**Pepino**	Concombre
Grapes	**Uvas**	Raïm
Melon	**Melón**	Meló
Mushrooms	**Champiñones**	Xampinyons (also *bolets*, *setes*)
Onions	**Cebollas**	Cebes
Orange	**Naranja**	Taronja
Potatoes	**Patatas**	Patates
Pear	**Pera**	Pera
Peas	**Arvejas**	Pèsols
Pineapple	**Piña**	Pinya
Peach	**Melocotón**	Préssec
Strawberries	**Fresas**	Maduixes
Tomatoes	**Tomates**	Tomàquets

Bocadillos fillings

ENGLISH	CASTILIAN	CATALAN
Catalan sausage	**Botifarra**	Butifarra
Cheese	**Queso**	Formatge
Cooked ham	**Jamón York**	Cuixot dolç
Cured ham	**Jamón serrano**	Pernil salat
Loin of pork	**Lomo**	Llom
Omelette	**Tortilla**	Truita
Salami	**Salami**	Salami
Sausage	**Salchichón**	Salxitxó
Spicy sausage	**Chorizo**	Xoriç
Tuna	**Atún**	Tonyina

Tapas and racions

ENGLISH	CASTILIAN	CATALAN
Anchovies	**Boquerones**	Anxoves
Stew	**Cocido**	Bollit
Squid, (usually deep-fried in rings)	**Calamares**	Calamars
Squid in ink	**Calamares en su tinta**	Calamars amb tinta
Snails, (often served in a spicy/curry sauce)	**Caracoles**	Cargols
Cockles (shellfish)	**Berberechos**	Cargols de mar
Whole baby squid	**Chipirones**	Calamarins
Meat in tomato sauce	**Carne en salsa**	Carn amb salsa
Fish or chicken croquette	**Croqueta**	Croqueta
Fish or meat pasty	**Empanadilla**	Empanada petita
Russian salad (diced vegetables in mayonnaise)	**Ensaladilla**	Ensalada russa
Aubergine/eggplant and pepper salad	**Escalibada**	Escalibada
Broad beans	**Habas**	Faves
Beans with ham	**Habas con jamón**	Faves amb cuixot
Liver	**Hígado**	Fetge
Prawns	**Gambas**	Gambes
Mussels (either steamed, or served with diced tomatoes and onion)	**Mejillones**	Musclos
Razor clams	**Navajas**	Navallas
Olives	**Aceitunas**	Olives
Hard-boiled egg	**Huevo cocido**	Ou bollit
Bread, rubbed with tomato and oil	**Pan con tomate**	Pa amb tomàquet
Potatoes in garlic mayonnaise	**Patatas alioli**	Patates amb all i oli
Fried potato cubes with spicy sauce and mayonnaise	**Patatas bravas**	Patates cohentes
Meatballs, (usually in sauce)	**Albóndigas**	Pilotes
Kebab	**Pincho moruno**	Pinxo
Octopus	**Pulpo**	Pop
Sweet (bell) peppers	**Pimientos**	Prebes
Kidneys in sherry	**Riñones al jerez**	Ronyons amb xeres
Sardines	**Sardinas**	Sardines
Cuttlefish	**Sepia**	Sípia
Tripe	**Callos**	Tripa
Potato omelette	**Tortilla española**	Truita espanyola
Plain omelette	**Tortilla francesa**	Truita francesa
Pepper, potato, pumpkin and aubergine/eggplant stew with tomato purée	**Tumbet**	Tumbet
Mushrooms (usually fried in garlic)	**Champiñones**	Xampinyons
Spicy sausage	**Chorizo**	Xoriç

LANGUAGE

Food and drink

Selected Balearic dishes and specialities

Many of the specialities that follow come from the Balearics' shared history with Catalunya. The more elaborate fish and meat dishes are usually limited to the fancier restaurants.

SAUCES

Mayonnaise	Salsa mahonesa
Garlic mayonnaise	Allioli
Spicy tomato and wine sauce to accompany fish (from Tarragona)	Salsa romesco

SOUPS (SOPA), STARTERS AND SALADS (AMANIDA)

Salad with sliced meat and cheese	Amanida catalana
Mixed meat soup	Carn d'olla
Starter of mixed meat and cheese	Entremesos
Aubergine/eggplant, pepper and onion salad	Escalivada
Mixed vegetable soup	Escudella
Spinach with raisins and pine nuts	Espinacs a la Catalana
Dried cod salad with peppers, tomatoes, onions and olives	Esqueixada
Baked vermicelli with meat	Fideus a la cassola
Stewed lentils	Llenties guisades
Bread rubbed with olive oil (eaten with ham, cheese or fruit)	Pa amb oli
Ratatouille-like stew of onions, peppers, aubergine/eggplant and tomato	Samfaina
Garlic soup	Sopa d'all
Vegetable soup, sometimes with meat and chickpeas garbanzos	Sopas mallorquínas
Omelette/tortilla (with garlic; with mushrooms; with potato). (Be sure you're ordering omelette (tortilla), not trout (truita).	Truita (d'alls tendres; de xampinyons; de patates)

RICE DISHES

"Black rice", cooked with squid ink	Arròs negre
Rice with seafood (the rice served separately)	Arròs a banda
Paella (rice with seafood and saffron)	Arròs a la marinera
Mixed meat and seafood paella (sometime distinguished from a seafood paella by being called Paella a Valencia)	Paella a la Catalana

MEAT (CARN)

Aubergines/eggplants stuffed with grilled meat	Albergínies en es forn
Spicy blood sausage with white beans	Botifarra amb mongetes
Rabbit (with garlic mayonnaise)	Conill (all i oli)
Chicken and potato stew in an almond sauce	Escaldum
Veal stew	Estofat de vedella

LANGUAGE Food and drink

Liver	Fetge
Veal casserole	Fricandó
Pigs' offal, potatoes and onions cooked with oil	Frito mallorquín
Meatballs, usually in a sauce with peas	Mandonguilles
Partridge in vinegar gravy	Perdius a la vinagreta
Chicken (stuffed; with prawns; cooked in sparkling wine)	Pollastre (farcit; amb gambas; al cava)
Pork (roast)	Porc (rostit)
Finely minced pork sausage, flavoured with paprika	Sobrasada

FISH (PEIX) AND SHELLFISH (MARISC)

Dried cod (with ratatouille)	Bacallà (amb samfaina)
Lobster stew	Caldereta de llagosta
Clams (often steamed)	Cloïsses
Turnover filled with spinach and eel	Espinagada de Sa Pobla
Fish and shellfish stew	Guisat de peix
Lobster (with chicken in a rich sauce)	Llagosta (amb pollastre)
Hake (either fried or grilled)	Lluç
Steamed mussels	Musclos al vapor
Octopus	Pop
Monkfish with creamed garlic sauce	Rap a l'all cremat
Fish and shellfish stew	Sarsuela
Fish casserole	Suquet
Trout (sometimes stuffed with ham, a la Navarre)	Truita

DESSERTS (POSTRES) AND PASTRIES (PASTAS)

Pastry containing vegetables and fish	Cocaroll
Crème caramel (with caramelized sugar topping)	Crema Catalana
Flaky spiral pastry, often (with fillings such as *cabello de ángel*) (sweetened citron rind)	Ensaimada
Curd cheese and honey	Mel i mató
Cake of dried fruit and nuts	Postres de músic
Almond fudge	Turrón
Deep-fried doughnut sticks (served with hot chocolate)	Xurros

Drinking

ENGLISH	CASTILIAN	CATALAN
Water	**Agua**	Aigua
Mineral water	**Agua mineral**	Aigua mineral
(sparkling)	**(con gas)**	(amb gas)
(still)	**(sin gas)**	(sense gas)
Milk	**Leche**	Llet
Juice	**Zumo**	Suc
Tiger nut drink	**Horchata**	Orxata
Coffee	**Café**	Café
Espresso	**Café solo**	Café sol
White coffee	**Café con leche**	Café amb llet
Decaf	**Descafeinado**	Descafeinat
Tea	**Té**	Te

Drinking chocolate	**Chocolate**	Xocolata
Beer	**Cerveza**	Cervesa
Wine	**Vino**	Vi
Champagne/Sparkling wine	**Champán/Cava**	Xampan/Cava

Glossary of Catalan terms

Town hall	Ajuntament
Lagoon (and surrounding wetlands)	Albufera
High altar	Altar major
Parking	Aparcament
Avenue	Avinguda (Avgda)
Bay	Badia
Ravine	Barranc
Baroque	Barroc
Catholic church with honorific privileges	Basílica
Small bay, cove	Cala
Way road	Camí
At the house of (contraction of *casa* and *en*)	Ca'n
Chapel	Capella
Street	Carrer(c/)
Road, highway	Carretera
Castle	Castell
Cellar, or a bar in a cellar	Celler
Cloister	Claustre
Col, mountain pass	Coll
Convent, nunnery or monastery	Convent
Post office	Correu
Caves	Coves
Church	Església
Small lake	Estany
Festival	Festa
Estate or farmhouse	Finca
Water fountain or spring	Font
Gothic	Gòtic
Island	Illa
Garden	Jardí
Lake	Llac
Market	Mercat
Watchtower or viewpoint	Mirador
Literally "Modernism", the Catalan form of Art Nouveau, whose most famous exponent was Antoni Gaudí; adjective *Modernista*	Modernisme
Monastery	Monestir
A Christian subject of a medieval Moorish ruler; hence Mozarabic, a colourful building style that reveals both Christian and Moorish influences	Mozarabe

A Moorish subject of a medieval Christian ruler. Also a style of architecture developed by Moorish craftsmen working for Christians, characterized by painted woodwork with strong colours and complex geometrical patterns; revived between the 1890s and 1930s and blended with Art Nouveau forms	Mudéjar
Museum	Museu
The Virgin Mary ("Our Lady")	Nostra Senyora
Tourist office	Oficina d'Informació Turística
Palace, mansion or manor house	Palau
Park	Parc
Boulevard; the evening stroll along it	Passeig
Summit	Pic
Square	Plaça
Beach	Platja
Bridge	Pont
Harbour, port	Port
Door, gate	Porta
Hill, mountain	Puig
Avenue or boulevard	Rambla
The Christian Reconquest of Spain from the Moors beginning in the ninth century and culminating in the capture of Granada in 1492	Reconquista
King	Rei
Royal	Reial
Queen	Reina
Iron screen or grille, usually in front of a window	Reixa
Rebirth, often used to describe the Catalan cultural revival at the end of the nineteenth and beginning of the twentieth centuries. Architecturally, this was expressed as *modernisme*.	Renaixença
Retable or reredos, a wooden ornamental panel behind an altar	Retaule
River	Riu
Pilgrimage or gathering at a shrine	Romeria
Saltpans	Salinas
Sanctuary	Santuari
Saint	Sant/a
Mountain range	Serra
Cone-shaped prehistoric tower	Talayot
T-shaped prehistoric megalithic structure	Taula
Stream or river (usually dry in summer)	Torrent
Modern estate development	Urbanització
Valley	Vall

"The most accurate maps in the world"

San Jose Mercury News

Information on over 25,000 destinations around the world

- **Read** Rough Guides' trusted travel info

- **Access** exclusive articles from Rough Guides authors

- **Update** yourself on new books, maps, CDs and other products

- **Enter** our competitions and win travel prizes

- **Share** ideas, journals, photos & travel advice with other users

- **Earn** points every time you contribute to the Rough Guide community and get rewards

BROADEN YOUR HORIZONS

small print & Index

SMALL PRINT

A Rough Guide to Rough Guides

In 1981, Mark Ellingham, a recent graduate in English from Bristol University, was travelling in Greece on a tiny budget and couldn't find the right guidebook. With a group of friends he wrote his own guide, combining a contemporary, journalistic style with a practical approach to travellers' needs. That first Rough Guide was a student scheme that became a publishing phenomenon. Today, Rough Guides include recommendations from shoestring to luxury and cover hundreds of destinations around the globe, including almost every country in the Americas and Europe, more than half of Africa and most of Asia and Australasia. Millions of readers relish Rough Guides' wit and inquisitiveness as much as their enthusiastic, critical approach and value-for-money ethos. The guides' ever-growing team of authors and photographers is spread all over the world.

In the early 1990s, Rough Guides branched out of travel, with the publication of Rough Guides to World Music, Classical Music and the Internet. All three have become benchmark titles in their fields, spearheading the publication of a range of more than 350 titles under the Rough Guide name, including phrasebooks, waterproof maps, music guides from Opera to Heavy Metal, reference works as diverse as Conspiracy Theories and Shakespeare, and popular culture books from iPods to Poker. Rough Guides also produce a series of more than 120 World Music CDs in partnership with World Music Network.

Visit www.roughguides.com to see our latest publications.

Rough Guide travel images are available for commercial licensing at www.roughguidespictures.com

Publishing information

This 2nd edition published April 2008 by Rough Guides Ltd, 80 Strand, London WC2R 0RL. 345 Hudson St, 4th Floor, New York, NY 10014, USA.

Distributed by the Penguin Group
Penguin Books Ltd, 80 Strand, London WC2R 0RL
Penguin Group (USA), 375 Hudson Street, NY 10014, USA
14 Local Shopping Centre, Panchsheel Park, New Delhi 110017, India
Penguin Group (Australia), 250 Camberwell Road, Camberwell, Victoria 3124, Australia
Penguin Group (Canada), 10 Alcorn Avenue, Toronto, ON M4V 1E4, Canada
Penguin Group (NZ), 67 Apollo Drive, Mairangi Bay, Auckland 1310, New Zealand
Typeset in Bembo and Helvetica to an original design by Henry Iles.

Cover concept by Peter Dyer.

Printed and bound in China
© Phil Lee 2008

No part of this book may be reproduced in any form without permission from the publisher except for the quotation of brief passages in reviews.
192pp includes index

A catalogue record for this book is available from the British Library

ISBN 978-1-85828-614-3

1   3   5   7   9   8   6   4   2

Help us update

We've gone to a lot of effort to ensure that the second edition of Mallorca DIRECTIONS is accurate and up-to-date. However, things change – places get "discovered", opening hours are notoriously fickle, restaurants and rooms raise prices or lower standards. If you feel we've got it wrong or left something out, we'd like to know, and if you can remember the address, the price, the phone number, so much the better.

Please send your comments with the subject line "Mallorca DIRECTIONS Update" to ✉mail@roughguides.com. We'll credit all contributions and send a copy of the next edition (or any other Rough Guide if you prefer) for the very best emails.
Have your questions answered and tell others about your trip at ⊕community.roughguides.com

SMALL PRINT

Rough Guide credits

Text editor: Nikki Birrell and Keith Drew
Layout: Ankur Guha
Photography: Suzanne Porter
Cartography: Ashutosh Bharti

Picture editor: Sarah Cummins
Proofreader: Jennifer Speake
Production: Rebecca Short
Cover design: Chloë Roberts

The author

Phil Lee has been writing for Rough Guides for well over ten years. His other books in the series include Canada, Norway, Amsterdam, England and Toronto. He lives in Nottingham, where he was born and raised.

Acknowledgements

Phil Lee would like to thank his editor, Nikki Birrell, for her patient and diligent work on this new edition of Mallorca – it was much appreciated. Special thanks also to Maria Peterson for all sorts of fact finding; Ilse Bock for her hospitality and advice; and George Scott for his help – and wit.

Readers' Letters

Thanks to all the readers who took the trouble to write and email in with their comments and suggestions and apologies if we've inadvertently omitted or misspelt anyone's name:

Jim Abercrombie; Jenny Aldous; Frances Allen; David Anderson; Dinah Anderton; Marcene Ansterberry; Marek Antoszewski; Jenny Atton; Billy Averall; Ann Bamforth; John Banfield; Jim Barrell; Bridget Beck; Miguel Bonet; Michael & Frances Bowerman; Mike Braide; Lynette Brucks; Derek Bryce; Stuart Bull; Philip Burnard; Rebecca & Natasha Burnham; Sarah Callan; Val Carlill; John and Midge Casset-ton; Angela and Matt Chapman; Chris Coakes; Sue Coats; V. A. Cooke; I. A. Cowie; Darrall Cozens; Jane Crawford-Baker; Damon Crawshaw; Anita Creed; Robert Crouch; Paul Davis; Mike Dean; Mark Dorrington; Kathryn Drewitt; Tove Elander; Alison Ewington; Graeme Falconer; John Fanshawe; Bettina Hartas Geary; Eri Gideon; John and Valerie Given; Anne Goodchild; Nick Gool; Annekatrin Grafton; Steven Graham; Mel Greig; Steve Hale; Nick Halsted; Nicola Hambridge; Roberta Heneage; Liz Heron; Karin von Herrath; Simon Hillyard; Nina Holmes; David Ireland; Pam and John Ireland; Malcolm Jackson; Tim Jenkins; Stuart Johnson; Lynn Tipper Jones; Hugh Josty; Susan Jurczyk; Hugh Kearney; Solna, Roger, J A Ketley; Elizabeth and Geoff Key; John Kop; Paul Lampard; John Landau; David Lee; Peter Lloyd; Roger Loxley; B. R. Lumby; Janet Macdonald; Yvonne McFarlane; Claire McGregor; Sian Mackay; Barbara McKiernan; Mary Marshall; Robbie Martzen; David Mather; Nicola and Ian Maunders; Phil Minshull; Andy Mitter; Clare and Richard Morgan; Lisa Nellis; David & Christine Neville; Hilary Nicol; Clive Paul; Chris Peake; Joan Pozzoli; Ann Roberts; Tony Robinson; Eric and Sally Rowland; Carol Saddington; H. H. Saffery; Helen Sandelands; George Scott; Judith de Serra; Jean Sinclair; David Sloan; Debbie Smith; Roxane Smith; Pat Stafford; Edward Staines; Wendy Stock; Zelda Tolley; Jan Trapmore; Barry Turner; Ann Viera; David Wallington; Christine Watson; Stephanie Webb; Wolfgang Weiss; M. Welch; John Weldon; E. Werenowska; Selina Westbury; Tom Whitehall; Clive Wilkin; Stephen Withers; Jean Woods; Claire Woodward-Nutt; Leesa Yeo.

Photo credits

All images © Rough Guides except the following:

Front cover picture: Orange trees in Sóller © Schmid Reinhard/4cornersimages

Back cover picture: Pine trees on the Peninsular de Formentor © Ellen Rooney/Axiom

Selected images from our guidebooks are available for licensing from:
ROUGHGUIDESPICTURES.COM

Index

Maps are marked in colour

190

INDEX